Table of Contents

Departments

2	**Old, Bold and Good as Gold** by Randall J. Strossen, Ph.D.
4	**Letters to the Editor**
37	**Calendar**
66	**Iron Filings**
68	**Captains of Crush® Grippers: Who's New**
69	**Red Nail™ Roster**
127	**The Iron Mine**

People

24	**The Sky's the Limit for Mike Zolkiewicz** by David W. Barron
61	**Stanless Steel: Man of Steel** by Mike Corlett

Training

16	**The Jo-Bar: A Small Barbell with Big Results** by Ken Best
19	**A Quick Summary of Strength Training in the Modern Age** by Dr. Ken E. Leistner
32	**CrossFit for Lifters?** by Adam Farrah
38	**Taking on the Steel Giant** by John Brookfield
40	**Advancing Punching Power through Variable Method Complexes** by Steven Helmicki
44	**Getting the Body Ripped and Toned in a Fast and Healthy Way** by Steve Justa
75	**King Beowulf and the Dragon's Lair: Are Your Ready?** by William Crawford, M.D.
80	**Overtraining—Symptoms, Causes, Prevention** by Ernest Roy P.T., D.P.T.
84	**Weightlifting and Blood Pressure** by Dezso Ban
89	**Foundations: Shoulder Pain? Join the Club** by Jon Bruney
96	**Three Lessons Learned from Jim Schmitz** by Darryl Jarman
100	**Customize Your Program to Fit Your Individual Needs** by Bill Starr
108	**Standing Weight-Over-Bar: A Primer Course** by Thom Van Vleck
124	**Fringe** by Steven Helmicki
124	**Harnessing the Power of Placebo** by Brian Jones, Ph.D.

Contests

5	**2009 World's Strongest Man: "The Right Man Won"** by Randall J. Strossen, Ph.D.
28	**2009 IAWA World Championships** by Roger Davis
46	**2009 World Weightlifting Championships: Lift the Limit** by Jim Schmitz
70	**Strength Contests at the Grass-Roots Level**
91	**Club Cal Neva Pro–Am Armwrestling Spectacular** by Denise Wattles
115	**2009 U.S. Invitational Heavy Events Championships and IHGF World Hammer Championships: Non-Stop Top-Flight Throwing** by Francis Brebner

History

87	**German Men of Might: Alois Selos** by Gherardo Bonini

Minutes before the finals in the 2009 World's Strongest Man contest began, Bill Kazmaier nodded toward Zydrunas Savickas and said to Randall Strossen, "If there's one man on the planet who deserves this title . . . " Zydrunas Savickas is strong in just about any way that you might reasonably assess strength—he's a proven player on overhead presses, squats and deadlifts, and yes, he'd won virtually every big strongman contest on the planet, so wasn't it about time that he won the biggest of them all, the World's Strongest Man contest?
Randall J. Strossen photo.

Old, Bold and Good as Gold

"**Y**outh is truth," is a popular view, at least in the West, but then others might add, "Too bad youth is wasted on the young."

The young—brimming with energy and starry-eyed views, kids barely out of college, maybe even still getting allowances from their mothers—are working in positions eagerly telling others how to run the world. "That's good," the seasoned might wryly say. "Be sure to tell everyone else what to do while you still know everything."

Old people—creaking in mind and body, not capable of much more than remembering the glory days—are convinced that they're the only ones in the room who know the truth. "Back in my day, we pressed strict and walked ten miles to school—and it was uphill, both ways."

Some place, though, there is the perfect balance, which requires a working familiarity with history: you might not need to know who won the super heavyweight title at the first official U.S. national powerlifting championships, let alone why the winning lift was suspect, but if you are asking, "Who's Tommy Kono?" you need to do some homework. Even if you don't own a full set of *Strength & Health, Iron Man* or *Lifting News* magazines, you can at least do some research at the level of checking online. And from the other direction, what's needed is a clear understanding that time marches on, with new growth cycles being the natural and inexorable order of things. Share your knowledge and experience with the next generation, and help to groom them as your worthy successors.

Infatuation with the splendors of youth while remaining blind to its frailties is not universal; in fact, some cultures put old age on a pedestal, equating it with wisdom, making it a necessary and sufficient basis for respect. The massive medical, pharmaceutical and cosmetics industries cater to a population deathly afraid of growing old—or at least looking old. Thus, they are certain to downplay the dictum "Respect your elders" in wealthy countries, and they actively reinforce the impression that aging is nothing short of despicable. But hang on, some old people have not been limited by these notions: they have superseded the stereotype.

Recently, the 104-year-old Joe Rollino was struck by a car and killed while walking across a New York street to get his daily newspaper. Joe, a fixture at AOBS dinners, in death as in life, drew in an admiring public, those who knew him as well as those who were just learning of him for the first time. Suddenly, everyone had been Joe's best friend, but the telling point is that here was a man who—just shy of his 105th birthday—aged with grace and dignity and for whom old age itself had become a huge asset.

Think about what it means to be over a century old. Ever plant a tree and watch it grow for even a decade or two? Now, pull back the camera for a wider view and think of your hometown, then your country, continent and the planet . . . how they have been transformed in that period of time.

Joe Rollino was like a tree planted way back then, adding rings each year, with each ring being a marker for all that had taken place in that slice of time—things that affected his life and others at that moment and things that would be encoded in his DNA, influencing the future with unassailable certainty. People like Joe Rollino are remarkable and they are vital, people who can bring the past to life in the present so that both can shape the future.

At least in the United States, we are trained to loathe any signs of aging and to cast the elderly in their expected roles, as merely the little old ladies and men that kind-hearted Boy Scouts safely guide across streets—but I urge you to give up that idea. Think of Joe Rollino, Jack LaLanne and even the relative youth Odd Haugen, instead. And above all, for inspiration, I would like to share my favorite of all the stories I've heard about another white-haired wizard, Karl Norberg.

When Karl was 79, he went to a casino with his daughter and her husband, and while watching someone gamble, Karl felt his pocket being picked. Reaching behind, Karl grabbed the offender by the wrist, turned around, lifted the guy overhead and shook him, saying, "It's not nice to pick on old people," and then Karl slammed the guy to the ground.

As ever, train safely, wisely and as hard as you can.

Randall J. Strossen, Ph.D.
Publisher & Editor-in-chief
Nevada City, California

Joe Rollino, at a mere 103 years old. Randall J. Strossen photos.

Published by IronMind Enterprises, Inc.

Randall J. Strossen, Ph.D.
Publisher & Editor-in-chief

Elizabeth M. Hammond
Production Editor

Susan Altman
Production Assistant

P.O. Box 1228
Nevada City, CA 95959 USA
www.ironmind.com
Tel: +1-530-272-3579
Fax: +1-530-272-3095
E-mail: sales@ironmind.com

MILO is published quarterly:
March, June, September &
December
Subscription rates for
4 books are:
Softcover: US$79.95/year USA;
US$89.95/year Canada/Mexico;
US$99.95/year all others
On-line:
US$42.95/year all subscribers

Single issues are:
US$20.00 each + $5.00 S&H USA
(US$7.00 S&H Canada/Mexico;
US$13.00 S&H all others)

Copyright ©2010
IronMind Enterprises, Inc.

All rights reserved.
No part of this publication
may be reproduced
or transmitted in any form
or by any means without prior
written permission except
in the case of brief quotations
embodied in articles
and reviews.

Design:
Tony Agpoon
Sausalito, CA

Letters to the Editor

Negative on Experiment

Brian Mangravite did a great job explaining the benefits of negative reps ("Accentuating the Negative," September 2009, Vol. 17, No. 2). [However] a penalty flag must be thrown at his example of bodybuilder Casey Viator adding 63 lb. of muscle in 28 days during the high-intensity training done in the so-called "Colorado Experiment" undertaken by Nautilus inventor Arthur Jones. If you read the study, you'll learn that immediately before the study began, Viator had lost more than 33 lb. as a result of physical inactivity due to a serious accident at work. Much of Viator's weight and muscle gain during the Colorado Experiment, then, was simply his body recovering, with the aid of intense training and a high-calorie diet, to what it was before the accident.

Moreover, the Colorado Experiment was not really an experiment at all—it essentially only had one subject (Viator). No one has come close to replicating Viator's reported experience despite the unaccountable number of athletes who have trained with weights during the last 36 years.
    Steve Milloy
    Publisher,
    JunkScience.com
    Potomac, MD

Caveman Training

I read with interest Steve Justa's "One-Arm Drag" article in MILO [September 2008, Vol. 16, No. 2] and have enjoyed the workout. Honestly, this exercise tugs at the human species' earliest origins when dragging a carcass back to camp or out of sight of other larger predators. Neat stuff!!
    Mark Viehweg
    Galesburg, IL

4 MILO | Mar. 2010, Vol. 17, No. 4

World's Strongest Man:

"The Right Man Won"

Randall J. Strossen, Ph.D.

Publisher & Editor-in-chief

All photos by Randall J. Strossen.

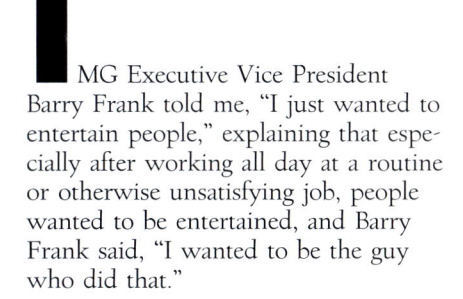

IMG Executive Vice President Barry Frank told me, "I just wanted to entertain people," explaining that especially after working all day at a routine or otherwise unsatisfying job, people wanted to be entertained, and Barry Frank said, "I wanted to be the guy who did that."

This is an understatement, coming from the man who has "negotiated some of the most lucrative sports television programming contracts ever signed," according to IMG. But provided massive entertainment he certainly has because the World's Strongest Man contest, Barry Frank's brainchild, has been viewed by an estimated tens of millions of people since it began in 1977.

"People like to see things they can't do—things that are extraordinary," Frank continued. "And strongman was like that."

It's hard to argue with Frank's point, because how many people can pull planes, lift huge stones, or deadlift cars?

Frank would also say that while he always expected each of his shows to be successful, he never really foresaw his TV show—*World's Strongest Man*—taking on the appearance of a quasi-sport, complete with warring federations.

Yet, with all the attempts to imitate, if not outdo, the World's Strongest Man contest, none has succeeded. With their history of coming up short year after year, fighting for second place or lower on the ladder, the wannabes only reinforce that World's Strongest

Man is the category killer, the mother of all strongman contests. "No matter what anyone says," Swedish strongman star Magnus Samuelsson told me at the 1997 World's Strongest Man contest, "this is the one we all want to win."

In 2009, World's Strongest Man (WSM) returned to Malta, the site of Jouko Ahola's 1999 victory. Malta is suitably exotic, a sun-drenched island in the middle of the Mediterranean, so all was set for the fun to begin.

The qualifiers shook down the initial field to the 10 hardies ready to move on:

1. Phil Pfister (USA)
2. Mariusz Pudzianowski (Poland)
3. Brian Shaw (USA)
4. Zydrunas Savickas (Lithuania)
5. Laurence Shahlaei (UK)
6. Travis Ortmayer (USA)
7. Louis- Philippe Jean (Canada)
8. Dave Ostlund (USA)
9. Terry Hollands (UK)
10. Derek Poundstone (USA)

Ten guys, or about 1-1/2 tons of human muscle, were ready to test their strength in ways that would rivet millions of eyeballs to their TVs worldwide.

Day 1

Day 1 started with Fingal's Fingers, long, heavy poles that are hinged at the bottom and have to be flipped. They progressed in weight—225 kg, 250 kg, 275 kg and 320 kg—and while you definitely have to be strong for this task, the best competitors will fairly fly through the course. Besides being strong and fleet of foot, to shine in this event it helps to be tall . . . but then, in this crowd being 2 m tall (about 6' 6") means you are just one of the guys.

Top three: 1) Zydrunas Savickas, 2) Dave Ostlund, and 3) Brian Shaw.

Next up was the Farmer's Walk, 160-kg per hand, up and back on a 25-m course. This event requires not just a strong back and set of legs, but also the kind of grip strength that can sustain the challenge. It also helps to be fast. Terry Hollands suffered badly ripped calluses on both hands from this event, but as you'd expect from the former rugby player turned strongman, that's no reason to throw in the towel. Top three: 1) Mariusz Pudzianowski, 2) Derek Poundstone, and 3) Brian Shaw and Travis Ortmayer (tied)

"What'd you do today, dear?"

"Pulled a jet."

That would be true if you were a 2009 World's Strongest Man competitor, as the Plane Pull was next. You'd think simply finishing the course would be tough enough, but the level of competition this year was such that the final results were decided by very slim margins of time. And Terry Hollands, undeterred by torn and bloody hands, won the *MILO*-guy award for having the most heart as he burned up the tarmac, posting the winning time. Top three: 1) Terry Hollands, 2) Zydrunas Savickas, and 3) Travis Ortmayer and Brian Shaw (tied).

Day 2

The Overhead Lift featured a thick bar fitted with large-diameter spoked wheels, the whole affair weighing in at 155 kg. Lifting styles varied, reflecting different strengths and degrees of technical proficiency, so while Zydrunas Savickas just pressed the bar overhead, Travis Ortmayer used a split jerk for the same purpose.

Coming back from a torn biceps, Dave Ostlund ripped through the Fingal's Fingers, going even faster than he did at WSM '08.

© RANDALL J. STROSSEN, PH.D.

Master of ceremonies Andy Quinn in his office.

© RANDALL J. STROSSEN, PH.D.

Barry Frank (l.), IMG Executive Vice President, is the father of World's Strongest Man, and Tim Kowalski (r.), is the show's producer.

Derek Poundstone (l.), who came into WSM '09 as a favorite, nips Terry Hollands (r.) at the line in the Farmer's Walk.

Star presenter Zoe Salmon gets her makeup adjusted before going on camera.

Ekaterina Majorskaya, of Russia's PLSE, was among the people who came to Malta to watch World's Strongest Man get filmed.

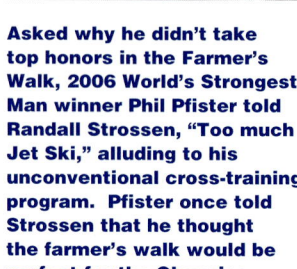

Asked why he didn't take top honors in the Farmer's Walk, 2006 World's Strongest Man winner Phil Pfister told Randall Strossen, "Too much Jet Ski," alluding to his unconventional cross-training program. Pfister once told Strossen that he thought the farmer's walk would be perfect for the Olympics.

Colin Bryce, longstanding WSM resource and head honcho of Giants Live!, the official qualifying tour of the World's Strongest Man contest.

He ripped the calluses on both hands in the first event, but don't think that took the wind out of Terry Hollands's sails because among other things, he went on to win the fiercely contested Plane Pull.

IMG event manager Lisa Comber.

Travis Ortmayer starts building up bad intentions for the Plane Pull . . . minutes later, with a rough start and a big pull behind him, he's up for air.

England's Laurence Shahlaei powers through the penultimate event, the Car Deadlift.

Martin "The Deadlift Kid" Wildauer made it to the qualifying round and then stayed around to watch the finals.

Wojtek Witkowski, Mariusz Pudzianowski's co-manager, does the photojournalist thing. Can you tell that Wojtek also manages rock musicians?

He is the face and voice of World's Strongest Man: Bill Kazmaier, a three-time winner and the very image of what a strongman competitor should look like.

If you're strong enough, as is Zydrunas Savickas, all you do to get the Axle overhead is stand there and press it.

Howard Woosey, the steadfast Steadicam man for WSM.

The Kaz commented on what an impressive job 5-time World's Strongest Man winner Mariusz Pudzianowski has done improving his performance on the Overhead Lift. Here, you can see that Pudzianowski used a push press to get the Axle overhead.

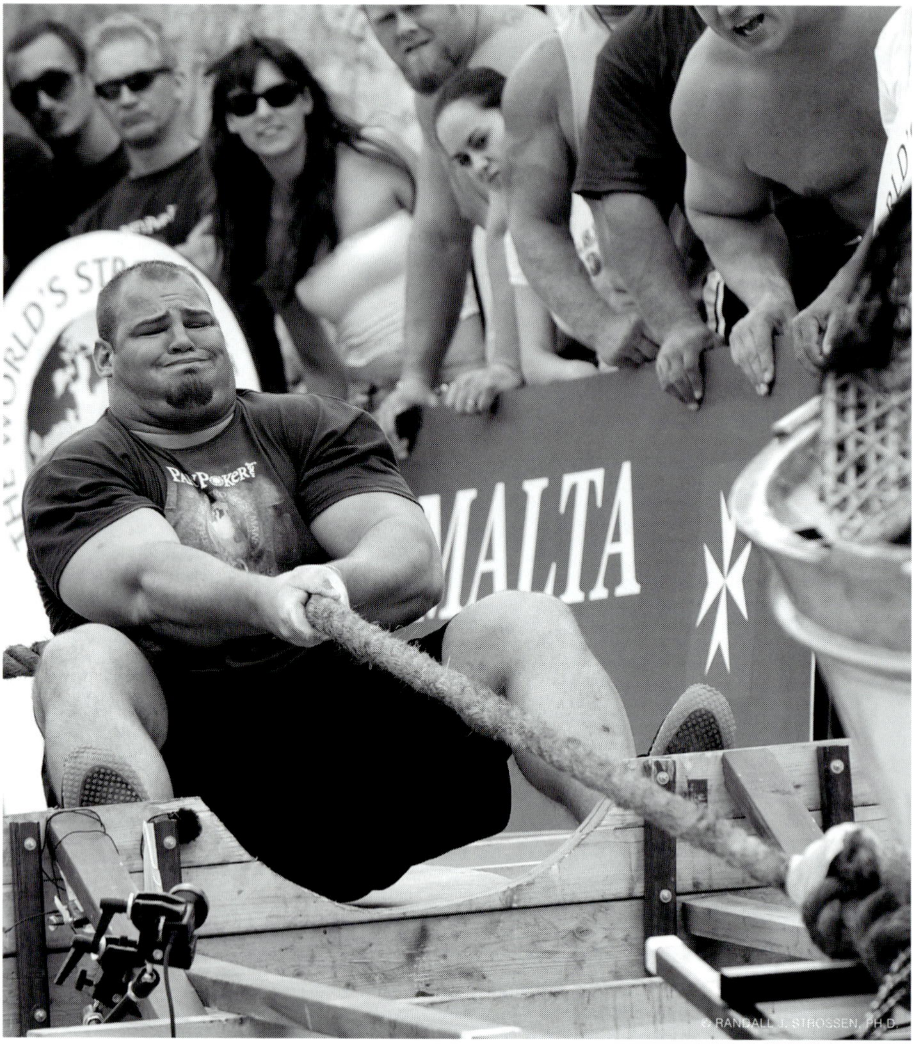

© RANDALL J. STROSSEN, PH.D.

Uphill, no water . . . no problem for Brian Shaw. Strongman floats his boat.

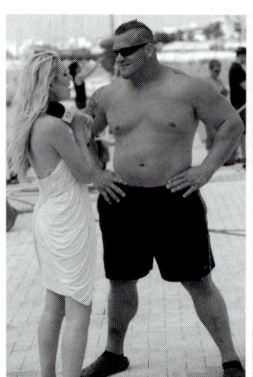

The never-shy Louis-Philippe Jean shares pleasantries with Zoe Salmon.

© RANDALL J. STROSSEN, PH.D.

© RANDALL J. STROSSEN, PH.D.

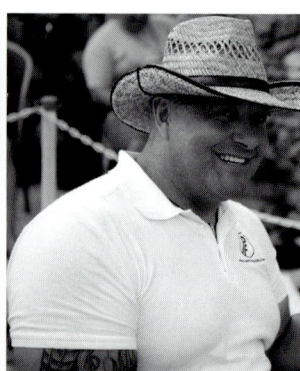

Svend Karlsen, 2001 World's Strongest Man winner, was on site working on the Norwegian TV version of the show.

Hugging it high on his chest, Dave Ostlund is about to place the final Atlas stone.

Louis-Philippe Jean shoulders a big stone and delivers it to its barrel.

Watch the start of the key matchup in the Atlas Stones . . . while Zydrunas Savickas still has not moved, Mariusz Pudzianowski has nearly flown over the first stone, quickly establishing a lead. But as the stones got heavier, Pudzianowski slowed down while Savickas was, well, rock-steady. When the Big Z put his final stone on its barrel and looked over to see how Pudzianowski was doing, what Savickas saw told him the story . . . he'd just won the 2009 World's Strongest Man title.

Bill Kazmaier told me that this was the event that made him a huge fan of Mariusz Pudzianowski, citing the progress Pudzianowski has made on the overhead lift in the last few years. Pudzianowski's preferred style? The push press. Top three: 1) Zydrunas Savickas, and 2) Derek Poundstone and Mariusz Pudzianowski (tied).

Next up was the Boat Pull, a rugged uphill arm-over-arm pull that saw the emergence of Brian Shaw as peerless at least on that day, setting the stage for calls of Shaw's future domination of strongman. Top three: 1) Brian Shaw, 2) Mariusz Pudzianowski, and 3) Travis Ortmayer.

Day 3

The deadlift is on anyone's list of key lifts for determining strength, but because this is the World's Strongest Man contest, simply using a standard barbell set isn't what the doctor ordered. Instead, enter the Car Deadlift, as cars are set up so that the competitors can hoist one end off the ground and see who can do the most reps. Straps are allowed and the weight at the bar was approximately 350 kg. Top three: 1) Zydrunas Savickas, and 2) Mariusz Pudzianowski and Derek Poundstone (tied).

The battle for the title was going to come down to the last event, the Atlas Stones, at 100, 110, 125, 140 and 160 kg. To win the title, Mariusz Pudzianowski would not only have to beat Zydrunas Savickas, but he would also have to have at least two competitors come between them, so that he could overcome the two-point deficit and Savickas's advantage on first place finishes.

Travis Ortmayer and Terry Hollands ripped through the course, with Ortmayer winning the heat and setting the fastest time to that point—a time that would hold up as the best in this event and as a new record, 24.2 seconds. Rock on, Texas Stoneman! Next, it was Brian Shaw beating Derek Poundstone, and then the big matchup: Zydrunas Savickas versus Mariusz Pudzianowski.

Shaw was guaranteed to be no worse that third overall at this point, but the most likely outcome was that Savickas and Pudzianowski would not be moving aside easily . . . one would win the title and the other would be second. Zydrunas Savickas, steady as ever, was unstoppable, and even the quick feet of Mariusz Pudzianowski were unable to match his pace. Top three in the stones: 1) Travis Ortmayer, 2) Zydrunas Savickas, and 3) Terry Hollands.

When all was said and done, Zydrunas Savickas had won the 2009 World's Strongest Man contest. Mariusz Pudzianowski was second, and Brian Shaw was third. **M**

> ZYDRUNAS SAVICKAS, STEADY AS EVER, WAS UNSTOPPABLE, AND EVEN THE QUICK FEET OF MARIUSZ PUDZIANOWSKI WERE UNABLE TO MATCH HIS PACE.

The Jo-Bar:
A Small Barbell with Big Results

Ken Best

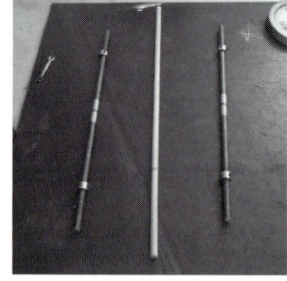

Japanese *jo* flanked by the home-made jo-bars.
Billy Best photos.

Sometime between 1602 and 1614, during the early Edo period in Japan, a young samurai named Muso Gonnosuke Katsuyoshi fought a sword duel with Miyamoto Musashi. At that time, Musashi was known as the best swordsman in Japan and had won many duels. Katsuyoshi was no slouch in the sword-fighting department either, having mastered the art of *ichi no tachi* (the sword of one cut); but on this day, he was defeated but left alive to contemplate his loss.

Legend says that Katsuyoshi went to Kamado Shinto shrine located on Mount Homan in Kyushu to meditate. Whilst there, he had a vision that told him to "seek the solar plexus with a round stick." He began to experiment with the *jo*, or stick, and came up with a number of techniques to defeat a sword. He called it *shindo muso-ryu jodo*. Once he mastered his new weapon, he challenged Musashi to a re-match. He won that match and went into the history books as being the only warrior to defeat Musashi—and he did it with a stick.

I trained in *shindo muso-ryu jodo* when I lived at the Sunshine Coast. I really enjoyed it and mastered the twelve *kihon*, or basic techniques, and still practice them today. It was during one of my practice sessions that I got the inspiration for the jo-bar. The *jo* is made from Japanese oak and is about 1.2 m (4 ft.) long and 25 mm (1 in.) in diameter. It is about 30 cm (almost a foot) longer than a samurai sword, giving its user the advantage of distance over the swordsman. Its big brother the *bo*, or staff, is about 1.8 m (6 ft.) long and resembles a barbell. I wondered what a barbell cut down to about the length of a *jo* would be like.

> He won that match and went into the history books as being the only warrior to defeat Musashi—and he did it with a stick.

I was short on funds at the time, so I purchased a 2-m (6-1/2 ft.) length of 25-mm (1-in.) diameter round bar and cut it in half. I secured two IronMind Bulldog II Collars to each bar, about 15 cm (6 in.) in from each end, and *voilà*, two jo-bars. In the tradition of *shindo muso-ryu jodo*, I have compiled a list of twelve exercises (*kihon*) I experimented with. At the time of writing this, I am getting good results and becoming stronger without injury.

1. Deadlifts: I use two jo-bars to perform parallel-grip deadlifts in much the same way I would use a trap-shrug bar. The advantage of the jo-bars is

that they require more wrist strength to prevent them from rocking forward and backward. It helps to mark them with tape and grip them at dead centre to reduce the rocking motion. One-arm versions are also good.

Parallel-grip deadlift with the jo-bar.

2. Shrugs: The jo-bars are ideal for shrugs. I can load them up and shrug them without the plates dragging on my legs. Hold a bar in each hand and shrug your shoulders to your ears. Bent-forward shrugs are also good, but you can't lean too far forward; otherwise, the rear plates rub your butt.

3. Upright rows: I prefer these over shrugs. In this lift, shrug and pull your elbows as high as you can whilst keeping a parallel grip. Paul Kelso calls these high pulls, and a picture of a lifter performing it can be seen on page 62 of his fantastic *Kelso's Shrug Book*.

4. Farmer's walk: Jo-bars are great for the farmer's walk. Once again, the plates are free of the legs, so the bars can be held comfortably at the sides. The rocking of the bars becomes more evident in this exercise, so tilt them down at the front to reduce this motion. Unlike other farmer's walk implements, which have handles to allow the weights to hang down, the jo-bars will try to twist out of your hands.

5. Pullover and press: The jo-bar is good for this exercise, particularly if

Ready to start the jo-bar farmer's walk

you use a close grip. It feels more secure than a barbell, because the plates are closer to you.

6. Overhead presses: I wasn't keen about using the jo-bars for this movement. They were hard to get into position, and the rocking motion threatened to cave in my skull. If you want to give presses a try, make sure you use very secure collars and be ready to dump the bars at any time.

7. Weighted sit-ups: A good application for the jo-bar, rest it across your chest and perform weighted sit-ups. The bar digs in a little, but that stops it from rolling onto your stomach or neck. I hold it on my chest with crossed hands to make sure it is secure, and I support some of the weight on my upper arms.

8. Hip belt squats: This is one of my favorites with the jo-bar. The weights are far enough away from your knees to allow deep squatting, but close enough to cut down on any rocking motion.

Hip belt squats with the jo-bar.

9. Calf raises: I follow a set of hip-belt squats with calf raises for a full leg workout. You arms are free to hang onto dipping bars for balance.

10. Curls: The jo-bar is about the same length as an EZ curl bar without the bends. You may find curling on the jo-bar better than an on EZ curl bar because your hands are supinated farther, which places more stress on your biceps.

11. Triceps extensions: Lying, seated, and standing triceps extensions all work well with the jo-bar. As with curls, the jo-bar allows for more pronation of the wrists, so you'll feel it more in the triceps. Close-grip bench presses are also good.

12. Weighted swings: A popular method of conditioning with martial artists these days is clubbell swinging. The act of swinging heavy clubs is as old as recorded history, but Coach Scott Sonnon has brought it into the present with his molded, heavy clubs, ranging from 2 to 20 kg. I load up the jo-bar with 20 half-kilo plates at one end, and perform slow swings and *jo* techniques as if I had a clubbell. The carry-over strength to my *jo* training is noticeable.

Jo-bar loaded with 10 kg in ready stance.

Here is the routine I am currently following. Note I still perform each session in strength-circuit format, where I complete all exercises in a row before having a short rest and doing it again.

Day 1: heavy – 3 circuits after warm-ups

- jo-bar deadlifts   3 x 6
- jo-bar sit-ups   3 x 12
- dumbbell bench presses   3 x 4
- neck harness   3 x 8
- dumbbell rows   3 x 4
- grippers   Trainer CoC x 15, No. 1 CoC x 4, No. 1.5 CoC x 4

Day 2: light

- re-hab/pre-hab exercises with bodyweight, cables and Swiss ball
- jo-bar swings 3 x 1 min. each direction (overhead, figure eight, front raises)
- jo-bar curls/extensions   1 x 10
- farmer's walk   x 50 m

Day 3: medium – 2 circuits after warm-ups

- jo-bar hip-belt squats   2 x 12
- jo-bar calf raises   2 x 12
- dumbbell presses   2 x 8
- dumbbell side-bends   2 x 8
- jo-bar shrugs   2 x 8
- grippers   Trainer CoC x 15, No. 1 CoC x 8

It's winter time here as I write this, hence the lower reps on Day 1. I like to train for strength during the colder months, as I suspect many MILO readers do. I follow each workout with 20–30 minutes of aerobic exercise in the form of machine rowing, skipping or hill walking. I do more *jodo* training on Saturday along with some other manual labor-type stuff, like digging, rock or log lifting, and sledgehammer swinging.

The jo-bar is inexpensive and simple to make. Be sure to use strong, secure collars, and lift on a forgiving surface in case you have to dump them. If you're adventurous, you could do the above exercises with two barbells, but be prepared for some serious wrist pain until you get used to them. **M**

A Quick Summary of Strength Training in the Modern Age

Dr. Ken E. Leistner
Chiropractor

My recent ramblings about the strength training that occurs specifically for football at both the university and professional levels could be summarized briefly, and some would say, brutally, as they do not agree with my assessment.

When the profession of strength coach was born, it was left primarily to active or former Olympic weightlifters who, predictably, generated programs that heavily emphasized Olympic weightlifting movements such as power cleans, overhead presses, and squats. As powerlifting became an organized sport and exceeded Olympic lifting in popularity, more former competitive athletes were drawn to the sport and most organized institutional strength training programs were then based upon the bench press, squat, and deadlift, in addition to some Olympic-style weightlifting movements. As the efficacy of well-designed training machines (specifically those manufactured by Nautilus) was embraced by many, some programs were either completely machine-based or predominantly machine-based. Over time, a combination of philosophies became the norm and most strength coaches utilized a variety of tools, sets, reps, and schemes to train their players.

During the initial stages of ascension and growth of the profession, the strength portion of strength and conditioning, if the term was used at all, was the province of the designated strength coach (who could have also been a full-time football coach whose staff designation was based upon the position he coached). For years there were defensive line coaches who served as *de facto* strength coaches. The conditioning part of training was left to the football coaches—either the head coach, who would plan specific technique and/or conditioning drills and the various running-related activities, or a member of the football staff who had a specific interest in that aspect of preparation.

In the early 1990s, more of the responsibility for preparing the team for its specific running needs was left to the strength coach, and it is rare to see an official designation for any professional in the field now read as "strength coach," as it is always "strength and conditioning coach." Unfortunately, whereas the actual strength-building work was overemphasized in the profession's early tenure, the pendulum has now swung to an extent where too much emphasis is placed on conditioning and what I have termed the "movement aspect" of training. There is now a de-emphasis on actually preparing players in a manner that will signifi-

> IT WILL SHOCK MANY FANS TO KNOW THAT ON SOME PROFESSIONAL FOOTBALL TEAMS, "THE LUNATICS RUN THE ASYLUM" . . .

cantly enhance their muscular size and strength over the three to five years they will be a part of the college football program.

In the pro ranks it is worse, as most coaches are hesitant and, in some cases, too timid to aggressively pursue a serious strength training regimen with their players for fear of injuring their multi-million dollar stars. It will shock many fans to know that on some professional football teams, "the lunatics run the asylum," with the players very much dictating to the strength and conditioning coaches what they desire to do in their workouts, and some eschewing the team workouts in favor of time spent with their personal trainers. If it's any solace, it's much worse in pro basketball.

All of this no doubt comes as a surprise to many typical MILO readers who are interested in athletics, football, and certainly strength training of any kind. Visions of the Pittsburgh Steelers' mid-1970s Super Bowl teams may come to mind, with a row of offensive linemen strolling up to the line of scrimmage, biceps straining the limits of their jersey sleeves and traps rolling up to their ears. Defensive linemen with taut, muscular quads and hamstrings bulging through the stretched material of their football pants could accompany the first image. Though the above may read as an advertisement for a steamy movie, it makes the point that most of us view football players who participate at the highest levels as being super strong and muscular freaks. Though many are, a majority of them do not lift weights often or with any semblance of serious intent. These men have been blessed with a superior muscular and neurological system that allows them their athletic success. They can perform physical feats we—mere fans who have not had the opportunity to stand on the field and actually experience their level of physical superiority—cannot even fathom.

> . . . WHEN A FAN YELLS, "THIS GUY STINKS," THAT PARTICULAR PLAYER IS STILL LIGHT YEARS AHEAD . . .

I have stated in previous articles through many decades that these guys are just not like you or me, and when a fan yells, "This guy stinks," that particular player is still light years ahead of wherever the screaming fan was as a high school or in-the-park-on-weekends player. The worst of them in the NFL (and in truth, the NFL of today, with its bloated roster numbers compared to the sparse pro rosters of the 1960s, has severely diluted its talent pool) still rise to the level of unbelievable and stupendous compared to anyone you might have played with in high school or in a bar league (unless they, too, were of major college or professional caliber). I can recall conversations about the Oakland Raiders' offensive line from a decade ago where a colleague noted, "Gee, they look like a group of fat guys getting ready to hit the local burger joint."

This particular set of offensive linemen did look like refugees from a cruise ship buffet table, but they were fat guys who were extremely skilled at the particular tasks unique to the positions they played and all had super-fast feet, great balance, and agility that allowed them to compete successfully in the NFL. Despite appearances, they were fully functional and excelled at the requirements of their specific positions because of unique physical gifts. As former Cincinnati Bengals strength coach Kim Wood used to state when watching a large, often fat lineman move like lightning, "Another Jackie Gleason," making reference to the entertainer of fifty-odd years ago who was rather heavyset, but also extraordinarily light on his feet and recognized as one of Hollywood's greatest dancers. The NFL-level players are very different physiologically and they are worth a lot of money! Thus, the strength and conditioning coach from the university level on up is saddled with the admonition, whatever you do, do not hurt them, do not cause a loss of practice or playing time, and do not bring a lawsuit to the program.

Strength and conditioning coaches have my utmost respect because they labor under conditions that are brutal in the best of circumstances. The hours are long to accommodate the players' needs and schedules. They have to be available to work around the schedules of the athletic trainers, physical therapists, medical doctors, and of course, the team coaches. Some are also charged with the responsibility of training the owner's family members. At the collegiate level, the strength coach is also a recruiter and a recruiting tool for the other staff members, and deservedly so. Unfortunately, it also means that they have to be available and to show the advantages of their weight room and philosophy to recruits and their families and high school coaches. When the other coaches are in a period of non-contact with players, the strength and conditioning coaches are the ones spearheading staff instructions and philosophies, training the players, and serving as their support system.

> STRENGTH AND CONDITIONING COACHES HAVE MY UTMOST RESPECT BECAUSE THEY LABOR UNDER CONDITIONS THAT ARE BRUTAL IN THE BEST OF CIRCUMSTANCES

When I have been asked by young aspirants in the field about becoming strength and conditioning coaches, I usually suggest that they explore other possibilities because the perceived glamour does not actually exist. With a level of education that is much higher than the public might guess and an investment of time and energy in what is usually at minimum a master's-level degree, one can avoid the reward-to-effort imbalance and the need to absorb a relatively high degree of abuse that many strength and conditioning coaches face.

As stated, my level of respect for the men and women who take on the responsibility of training athletes for the satisfaction of seeing them improve is enormous. To do so with the primary goal of placing the best conditioned and strongest team on the field, while answering to a multitude of others with agendas that often are at odds with each other, is difficult at best and sometimes impossible in the real-world setting of college or professional athletics. M

The Routine

Dr. Ken E. Leistner

I usually include a typical training program with the various articles I cover. It consists of basic movements and is brief in both volume and frequency relative to what most coaches and strength trainers recommend, but has a legacy of efficacy. Here is what might be termed a blast from the past that was initially presented in Dr. Ellington Darden's rather rare and extremely underrated book *Conditioning for Football*, published in 1979. As the mouthpiece and certainly the disseminator of the written word for Nautilus Sports/Medical Industries, Dr. Darden's many publications sang the praises of the Nautilus party line of training and the following program, one specifically for football, was no different.

Recognizing that the best way to prepare football players for combat was to take the raw material of the body—the skeletal-muscular system—and enhance size and strength through intense, hard, brief training, and then teach them the specific skills to actually play football, the program still has merit. Because it is machine-based, and please note my commentary regarding the substitution of a barbell or dumbbell exercise, it will be different for most readers of *MILO* who favor Olympic weightlifting, powerlifting, and strongman-type training. However, meeting the requirements for hard and intense training as well as adequate rest and recovery, this recommended regimen from 1979 retains its effectiveness and merit.

As one of a number of basic Nautilus workouts that provide variety in the movements and machines used, this one is typical and effective. The hip and back exercise was performed on a number of different generations of machines, all designed to directly work the hips and low back while avoiding the linear compression of doing barbell squats. Because the hip and back machine did not involve the quadriceps, leg extensions were done and immediately followed by leg presses and then leg curls, all with no rest between the movements.

Basic Nautilus workout 1

Hip and back machine
Leg extension
Leg press
Leg curl
Calf raise
Pullover
Pulldown
Arm cross on double chest machine
Decline press
Neck and shoulder (shrug)
4-way neck
Rotary neck

The demanding work done by the largest muscle groups of the body would leave the trainee in a state of breathlessness and obviously provide stimulation for the extremely important muscles relative to the sport of football. The effect was to directly work the squatting muscles and utilize a pre-exhaust method to give an even higher order of work to the lower extremities. I always preferred a combination of the barbell squat and stiff-legged deadlift for this purpose, but for those athletes who would not squat effectively for any reason, the hip and back was a misunderstood and underutilized tool. The calf or heel raise is not done by many high school, college, and professional strength programs, and the result is an expanded risk of ankle injuries.

The same comments as for the hip and back machine can be applied to another Nautilus movement, the pullover. One wants to work muscle tissue, and the pullover exercise was a staple in the gyms of the 1950s and 1960s because it affected the lats/upper back, pectorals, triceps, and serratus group. Described by Arthur Jones, the inventor of Nautilus, as the upper-body squat, the pullover's limitations as done with a barbell, either stiff-armed or bent-armed, were eliminated with the development of the pullover machine, which provided a range of motion otherwise impossible with a barbell. Combined with the close grip lat pulldown to the chest with a supinated grip, the large expanse of musculature in the upper back was stimulated, a key area to absorb force when making contact on the football field.

The arm cross or flye, though seen as a bodybuilding maneuver by lifting purists, actually works the primary function of the pectoral muscles—that of adducting the humerus, something the bench press does not match. The decline press follows on the double chest machine that combines the two exercises; this movement involves pre-exhaustion and also the stimulation of a lot of muscle tissue. The Nautilus decline press allows for a much broader and safer range of motion than a barbell or dumbbell bench press or decline press, and the flye-type movement is more controlled on a machine than with dumbbells.

For proponents of "I don't like guided resistance; the antagonists and so-called small muscles don't get the work needed," remember please that safety is a real issue and efficiency in movement also ranks high. The Nautilus equipment covers these factors, and there is ample opportunity to allow for small muscle work doing a lot of other exercise movements. The neck and shoulder, or shrug, machine is a no-brainer in any program that prepares athletes involved in contact sports. Of course, to truly specialize on that vital cervical spine region, this specific program also has work on the 4-way neck machine, and rarely seen rotary neck, but it is giving the emphasis where it is needed.

I have written volumes on the necessity of specific work for the cervical spine and trapezeii area to best prepare football players. Darden's program would receive an A+++ rating for giving this necessary work. Of course, I believe that one needs a specifically-designed neck machine for every football player.

Darden's other programs are just as basic, but in all, the emphasis is on full-body work performed to a point of momentary muscular failure/fatigue combined with adequate rest and recovery—still the right combination for muscular growth. ∎

> THE NECK AND SHOULDER, OR SHRUG, MACHINE IS A NO-BRAINER IN ANY PROGRAM THAT PREPARES ATHLETES INVOLVED IN CONTACT SPORTS.

The Sky's the Limit for
Mike Zolkiewicz

David W. Barron

The 56-lb. weight-for-height holds a unique spot in the annals of strength sports. An iconic event for centuries in the Scottish Highland Games, it has more recently become a staple of modern strongman competitions. Known variously as the Gaelic deadweight, the weight-for-height, and the weight-over-the-bar (or WOB), the event is one of the purest tests of power in either sport, and the few individuals to have laid claim to the record books have been some of the most powerful athletes ever to walk the earth. Such legends of the iron game as Bill Kazmaier, Geoff Capes, Ben Plucknett, Shannon Hartnett, Wout Zijlstra, and Matt Sandford have all made their mark in the event, delivering performances remembered years after the fact.

But now Mike Zolkiewicz, a professional Highland Games athlete from Springfield, Massachusetts, has surpassed them all. On July 18, 2009, at the International Highland Games Federation (IHGF) World Team Championships held in Antigonish, Nova Scotia, Mike set a new world record by clearing a height of 18' 9" in front of six thousand cheering spectators.

Anyone who had been following the accomplishments of the 6' 4" 285-lb. athlete knew that the record was in serious jeopardy. In May, Mike had cleared 18' 4", breaking the 16-year-old American record in the weight for height held by the late discus-throwing legend Ben Plucknett. Less than a month later, he cleared 18' 5" at the Kansas City Scottish Highland Games.

Mike is a 32-year-old personal trainer and strength and conditioning coach, and the owner of PowerClean Fitness in Massachusetts. A former over 200-ft. discus thrower, Mike competed in his first Highland Games at Goshen, Connecticut in 1997, thanks to the influence of Southern Connecticut State University throws coach Bill Sutherland. Mike didn't compete again until 2001 due to ACL (anterior cruciate ligament) replacement surgery, but he started competing professionally in 2003 and quickly established himself as one of the top throwers in the country. In 2007 Mike won the North American Championships Games in Enumclaw, Washington, and became the first American in a generation to clear 18' with the 56-lb. weight.

MIKE DISCOVERED EARLY ON THAT HE HAD A GIFT FOR THROWING THINGS REALLY FAR.

Mike discovered early on that he had a gift for throwing things really far. While playing at a friend's house (whose father happened to be a throwing coach), they found a discus and went outside to throw it. That very day Mike threw farther than the existing local junior high school record in the event. Mike was just ten years old. From then on, throwing was a fascination for him: "My first and biggest hero was Al Oerter. I learned all about what his lifts were, how strong he was. I trained off of that for a long time."

While he is clearly the best in the world right now at throwing the weight-for-height, Mike is also consistently one of the best stone putters on the field, thanks to his strong track and field background (he threw the shot over 58' in college). Mike is also one of the most accomplished caber tossers in the Games, having turned some of the longest and heaviest cabers (a born showman and ladies' man, Mike's signature event is throwing the caber without a shirt).

His best event results in the other traditional Highland Games are:

If you're good, you don't throw with your arms, but Mike has both: big arms and big throws.
Randall J. Strossen photo.

Braemar Stone	42' 4"
Open stone put	55' 4"
Heavy weight-for-distance	44' 6"
Light weight-for-distance	88' 0"
Heavy hammer	103' 2"
Light hammer	128' 7"
20-lb. sheaf	32'

Mike's list of heavy events accomplishments includes:

2003 World Amateur Shootout Champion
2007 1st place, North American Championships, Enumclaw, WA
2007 4th place, Highlander World Championships
2008 5th place, IHGF World Championships, Bridgeport, WV
2009 2nd place, Highland Games World Team Championships, Antigonish, NS
2009 6th place, U.S. Championships, Bethlehem, PA

Mike sends the 28-lb. weight-for-distance into orbit in Portland, Oregon.
Courtesy of David Barron.

> . . . MIKE STARTED SPENDING LESS TIME IN THE GYM, WHILE GETTING STRONGER AND "NOT FEELING NEARLY AS BEAT UP AS I HAVE IN PAST YEARS."

In training to set the weight-for-height record, Mike feels that the most important change was moving away from full Olympic movements and instead using variations such as hang cleans and hang snatches. "I didn't realize how important they were until I saw a video of (2008 world champion) Sean Betz hit a 380-lb. hang clean. I said, wow, I'm missing something big." Mike enlisted the help of Dr. "Rock" Bill Crawford to improve his lifting technique and to use the partial Olympic movements to help him become a better athlete.

"That was a huge turning point for me," Mike commented. Armed with his new training approach and with guidance from mentor–coach Jim Glassman, Mike started spending less time in the gym, while getting stronger and "not feeling nearly as beat up as I have in past years."

He squats 590 lb., and has front squatted 425 lb., benched 420 lb., done a 385-lb. clean, and snatched over 250 lb. He also lays claim to a 720-lb. deadlift (which shouldn't surprise anyone who's seen Mike's massive spinal erectors and long arms). While his weight room numbers won't impress many top-level powerlifters, Mike is one of the most athletic strength competitors you'll find in the U.S., having placed high in international strongman–Highland Games hybrid competitions in Scotland. In fact, there is no other American who competes at such a high level in both sports. Mike has won events against some of the strongest men in the world, including Mark Felix, Johannes Arso, Dan Ford, and Sebastian Wenta. "Any event that involves more than brute strength and requires some athleticism gives me a big advantage," says Mike. More impressive is the fact that, while he can match just about any professional strongman in events like farmer's walk or the medley, he has yet to dedicate a full season of training for strongman competitions.

In fact, Mike only trains in the strongman events for variety during the off-season from Highland Games. "It's a great way to find out where I am and where the weak points are in my lifting. The functional (strongman) training gets you stronger than anything I can do in the gym. I have become less injury-prone since I started training strongman events and have worked it into my Highland Games training. There is something about the 'shock' factor that you don't get anywhere else."

Mike Zolkiewicz wings the 56-lb. weight-for-height while competing in Burntisland, Scotland.
Courtesy of Winston Hatta.

Mike is determined to reach the top of the podium both in Highland Games and in the increasingly popular hybrid events, such as the New Hampshire Strongman Games and the Highlander Challenge, two international-level events where he has vied for top honors. Now injury-free and enjoying a solid off-season of getting stronger and training for the heavy events, there's no telling what Mike will accomplish in 2010.

As he proved in Nova Scotia, the sky's the limit. M

Catching up in the New Year with Kent Durso

"And lo, it came to pass that I didst go up amongst the giants, in the ninth month of the Romans, to the citadel of York, and though I couldst not carry off the city gates, I stretched forth my hand against the barbell and didst conquer it . . . sort of."—Letter of Kent to the Milonians, verse 1.

Actually, I was fairly well embarrassed at the York, Pennsylvania American Masters' Weightlifting Champion-ships on 7–8 November (remember, *novem* comes from the Latin word meaning nine, the ninth month of the Romans is therefore our eleventh); I made only three of six and my plan for a respectable 200-kg total was out the window. Still, I won by 50 kg over the next fellow and had the photo to prove it . . . but left it in the rental car in Baltimore.

Because of the reduced mobility in my shoulder, I had to use the split style and had real trouble with it, the opposite of what Jim Schmitz postulates (leave it to me to be backward). So, unable to properly rack the weight, I missed two jerks after easy power cleans and, well, that's my story and I am sticking to it. I am not publicizing the lifts because I don't want Ron Sisk of Lenexa, Kansas, a certified judge, to give me any more hell than I have already gotten from several Highlanders of ill repute.

I am planning on having a big 2010, as I turn 65. If I can rediscover the squat snatch, I plan to enter the Masters' Weightlifting Nationals in New York in April; if my wife doesn't divorce me, I will enter the Scottish Masters' Worlds in Denver in August, moving up an age group and hoping to lay waste to my competition once and for all.

So let me take this chance to wish you the happiest of New Years, one of prosperity and achievement, not to mention peace of mind on Earth to men and women of good will.
 Kent Durso
 Franklin, TN

IAWA World Championships

Roger Davis

As a follow-up to my recent all-round articles in MILO, I wanted to share with you the results from the International All-round Weightlifting Association (IAWA) World Championships, which were held this year in Lebanon, Pennsylvania, on 3–4 October and promoted by Denny Habecker. This was my last year as a senior lifter, before I turn 40, and I was determined to make these championships. The recession and relatively poor support from the host country led to a limited turnout, but to my mind, what was lacking in numbers was made up for in camaraderie and quality of lifting.

I shall report the highlights and results of the lifting, but more than that, I wanted to give you a few examples of the great atmosphere that exists in drug-free all-round weightlifting. It was upon my arrival at the venue that I met John Monk, who explained to me that he couldn't lift on the second day as he was coaching a group of special-needs lifters in a powerlifting competition. It was with some disappointment that I told John that that was a shame, as he was one of the lifters whom I was looking forward to competing against the most. John then decided to obtain permission to complete all 7 lifts on the first day to support the competition and give me the challenge I wanted, while still meeting his coaching responsibilities the next day. By the end of the day he was flagging and his lifts must have suffered from this schedule, but he had made up his mind that he wanted to support the competition.

> THE GAUNTLET HAD BEEN THROWN DOWN AND IT PROMISED TO BE A GREAT BATTLE BETWEEN THE BIG BOYS.

Day 1

The first lift of the day was the single-hand Hack lift, which involves lifting the bar from behind you with one hand—it puts a real strain on the obliques and is a very challenging lift. Big Al Myers managed 150 kg on this lift to just pip Mark Haydock's 145 kg and Chad Ullom's 140 kg. The gauntlet had been thrown down and it promised to be a great battle between the big boys.

The second lift was the clean and press behind the neck, a lift much more familiar to the athletes. Some of the lighter lifters were able to show a better lift-to-bodyweight ratio than the big boys—John Monk lifted 75 kg and I managed 80 kg. Very impressive were Denny Habecker with a 65-kg lift at 67 years of age, and Scott Schmidt, who showed a great press technique that demonstrated his Olympic weightlifting background, with 92.5 kg. Mark Haydock managed the heaviest lift of the day, 105 kg.

The third lift was the straight-arm pullover. This is a very difficult leverage lift, whereby the lifter lies on the floor and pulls the bar overhead from behind with straight arms, using discs of a maximum 11" in diameter. John Monk did 47.5 kg, Bill Spayd and Chad Ullom got 55 kg, and Mark Haydock raised this to 57.5 kg, only to be topped by 60 kg from Al Myers.

The final lift to tax the flagging lifters was the Ciavattone deadlift. The lift is a standard deadlift, but it is performed with a front knuckle grip and no hooking, and it was named after big Frank Ciavattone from Boston, one of the most naturally strong and biggest-hearted guys you could ever hope to meet. Frank holds the over-40 IAWA world record on this lift, with a very impressive 238 kg at +125 kg bodyweight, but it was the gesture that he was to make on this lift that in my mind really set him apart as a giant among men. Frank recently had had a hip replacement so he was making token lifts just to keep the others company, but the Ciavattone deadlift afforded him an opportunity to show off a bit of the old Frank.

Taking a final lift of 182.5 kg, Frank stood up straight, looked directly at the crowd, and said, "My name is Frank Ciavattone. Three months ago I had a hip replacement, thirty years ago I beat cancer, and I would like to dedicate this lift to my good friend Karen Gardner, who has just overcome her own personal battle with cancer. This lift is for you, Karen." Frank then gently and very slowly lowered the bar to the ground with a grip that remained rock solid. At how many weightlifting competitions do you see such acts of inspiration? It was a privilege to be there.

A number of lifters went over the 200-kg mark, including Bill Spayd, Chad Ullom, and Al Myers—but Mark Haydock made the top lift of the day with 227.5 kg.

Day 2
The first lift of the second day was the single-hand barbell snatch, which added a little bit of speed and dynamics to a program that had mainly consisted of static strength lifts. It was interesting to watch the technique differences, with the majority of U.S. lifters using the power snatch and the U.K. lifters using a full split snatch. I was pleased to get an equal personal best of 60 kg on this lift, but this was overshadowed once again when the big boys did battle by an impressive 80 kg by Mark Haydock, finishing off things.

The second lift was the pullover and press, basically a bench press performed without a bench. The hardest part of this lift is pulling over the bar onto the chest. Some very good lifts were performed, and among the best in my opinion was John Monk's 125-kg lift at less than 80 kg bodyweight. The top lift of the day was 160 kg by Al Myers, which just nosed ahead of Mark Haydock's 157.5 kg.

Talk about leaving the worst until last—the Zercher lift is an incredibly hard lift, performed by first lifting the bar from the floor to the knees, and then standing upright with the bar in the crooks of the elbows. The pain is epic.

Photos courtesy of Roger Davis

1. Al Myers on the single-arm Hack lift.
2. Frank Ciavattone on his eponymous deadlift.
3. Chad Ullom's single-arm snatch.
4. John Monk's single-arm snatch.
5. Art Montini on the Zercher lift.
6. Mark Haydock with a big Zercher lift.

Two performances that impressed me were the 85-kg and 77.5-kg lifts performed by Dennis Mitchell (77 years old) and Art Montini (81 years old), respectively. How many gentlemen of these advanced years do you know who could lift that weight from the floor, let alone stand up with the bar in the crooks of the arms? I was pleased with my 170 kg; I had hoped for a bit more but had messed up my second attempt as the barbell rolled off my legs. Josh Haydock's 137.5-kg lift at only 67 kg bodyweight was also worthy of mention.

> I DON'T THINK HE WAS TOO DISAPPOINTED AS HE HAD DRAWN A LARGE SMILEY FACE IN CHALK ON HIS LEOTARD BEFORE THE ATTEMPT!

Bill Spayd lifted 170 kg, Al Myers 190 kg, and Chad Ullom 200 kg, but big Mark Haydock was waiting in the wings and watching. He had calculated down to the last kilo what he needed to take home the victory to the U.K., and he came forth with an outstanding and comfortable 230 kg. Mark made a final record attempt with 250 kg, but it was not to be. I don't think he was too disappointed as he had drawn a large smiley face in chalk on his leotard before the attempt!

I hope you enjoyed this report on the two days of all-round lifting, but more importantly I hope you have been inspired by the people who lift in the IAWA. If you have set your sights on being a world-class Olympic lifter or powerlifter, I would stay focused on those lifts exclusively and do not deviate from your goals. If, however, you are looking to challenge yourself across a whole range of lifts in a drug-free and uplifting environment, I say you could do a lot worse than to join the IAWA and participate in the all-round competitions. Who knows, you may be the one to provide the inspiration at the next one!

For more information, contact websites www.usawa.com and www.iawa.org.uk.

IAWA World All-round Weightlifting Championships—Results
3–4 October 2009

Name	Country	Bwt	Age	OH Hack Lift	Clean & Press BN	Strt Arm Pullover	Ciavattone Deadlift	OH Snatch	Pullover & Press	Zercher Lift	Age/Bwt Total	Amended
Mark Haydock	UK	122.9	34	145	105	57.5	227.5	80	157.5	230	1002.5	764.3
Al Myers	USA	114.7	43	150	90	60	210	70	160	190	930	763.1
Chad Ullom	USA	104.3	37	140	90	55	205	70	145	200	905	749.7
Roger Davis	UK	81.6	39	117.5	80	45	185	60	120	170	777.5	738.4
Denny Habecker	USA	86.1	67	90	65	32.5	140	35	95	95	552.5	661.1
John Monk	USA	79.8	43	100	75	47.5	122.5	50	125	137.5	657.5	658.2
Bill Spayd	USA	107.9	35	110	90	55	200	60	120	170	805	655.2
Scott Schmidt	USA	119.7	56	100	92.5	40	182.5	40	92.5	115	652.5	598.5
Art Montini	USA	78.2	81	60	32.5	27.5	105	20	60	77.5	382.5	588.9
Josh Haydock	UK	66.9	19	72.5	55	25	132.5	37.5	70	137.5	530	582.1
John Kavanagh	UK	94.3	21	80	82.5	30	170	52.5	105	140	660	577.1
George Dick	UK	127.4	60	102.5	60	30	175	40	90	120	617.5	559.7
Dennis Mitchell	USA	72.1	77	50	20	20	90	15	35	85	315	484.4
Dennis Vandermark	USA	92.5	56	75	0	30	130	22.5	60	110	427.5	442
Kohl Hess	USA	118.8	15	82.5	42.5	27.5	120	30	60	80	442.5	394.4
Frank Ciavattone	USA	127.0	54	90	20	15	182.5	20	25	20	372.5	321.3

M

CrossFit for Lifters?

Adam Farrah

Author of *Practical Paleolithic*;
CrossFit Level 1 certified coach;
IKFF certified kettlebell teacher;
and owner of CrossFit Middletown
in Middletown, Connecticut

CrossFit is both a training philosophy and a sport and it will enhance anyone's training. Some, like myself, consider themselves "CrossFitters" and use CrossFit as the context within which to train things like power and Olympic lifts, agility, kettlebells, running, odd object lifting, and flexibility. CrossFit methodology can also be used as a training tool to enhance more focused or sport-specific training. CrossFit just plain makes you better at whatever it is that you do. This is one reason it's so popular among the military and first responders.

One thing CrossFit does exceptionally well is add an intensity component to workouts. The high intensity "met con" (metabolic conditioning) work wasn't invented by CrossFit, but I think they've perfected it and elevated it to someplace it's never been before. All serious CrossFitters pretty much demand crazy intensity in any workout you give them. It becomes addicting.

> CROSSFIT JUST PLAIN MAKES YOU BETTER AT WHATEVER IT IS THAT YOU DO.

I'm going to tell you how to selectively and occasionally (just 1 to 2 times per week) incorporate CrossFit methods into your existing routine to increase your training intensity dramatically. This type of intensity has a profound effect on aerobic or cardio conditioning and will give you an overall increase in fitness, strength, energy, and well-being. It will help you burn bodyfat and make your metabolism more efficient—all with a very short workout time and without having to get near a treadmill or stepper.

Quite simply, CrossFit will make you a better lifter. I promise.

What is CrossFit?

Functional movements, constantly varied, done at high intensity—that's the essence of CrossFit. If you lose "constantly varied," you basically have any good weight training program, be it powerlifting, Olympic lifting, or whatever. Are 20-rep squats with 315 lb. a functional movement done at high intensity? I would say so. What about a 275-lb. curl with a 2.5-in. bar? Probably. Farmer's walk with heavy dumbbells or kettlebells? Yes. Turkish get-up with a sandbag? Sure.

I believe the CrossFit methodology is exceptional because, among other things, it recognizes—and provides a framework for using—the fact that "anaerobic training can match endurance training for aerobic benefit." (1) This is an absolutely profound statement in its simplicity and elegance. What it means is that you can increase your cardiovascular capacity without doing traditional cardio training.

> THERE'S A JOKE AMONG CROSSFITTERS. PEOPLE ALWAYS LOOK AT A CROSSFIT WORKOUT AND ASK, "WHERE'S THE CARDIO?"

There's a joke among CrossFitters. People always look at a CrossFit workout and ask, "Where's the cardio?" It's a joke because: 1) CrossFitters don't use the traditional modes of cardio training for the most part, and 2) if you've ever done a CrossFit workout, you'd never, ever ask that question. CrossFit workouts are extremely challenging cardiovascularly. You won't really appreciate this fully until you're in the middle of your first one.

So, here's what we're going to do:

1. Take full advantage of the fact that anaerobic-style training can confer aerobic benefits when trained using CrossFit methods.

2. Use CrossFit principles to periodically and dramatically increase your training intensity.

3. Use CrossFit principles to accomplish a high number of repetitions of chosen movements in a compressed time interval.

The third point provides an opportunity to practice movements and consolidate form at a much lighter weight than usual—while keeping intensity very high.

CrossFit and benchmarking
There's another reason to include the CrossFit approach in your training. It gives you an opportunity to benchmark your fitness and objectively track your progress beyond just tracking poundage increases. This can be very valuable data for your training.

CrossFit did something revolutionary: it defined fitness. I won't go into all the particulars of how CrossFit defines fitness and what it all means, but I'd refer you to the article "What is Fitness?" on CrossFit.com for more information. (2)

As a lifter, you know that lifting a heavier weight than you did previously means you got stronger. In CrossFit, we recognize and embrace that. In CrossFit we also acknowledge that lifting the same weight in less time than before equates to an increase in fitness. For example, say you added 20 lb. to your 1-RM in the bench press. But, say that you also took unlimited rests between sets—more than ever before. You could definitely say you got stronger, but you would not necessarily be able to say you got fitter.

> YOU COULD DEFINITELY SAY YOU GOT STRONGER, BUT YOU WOULD NOT NECESSARILY BE ABLE TO SAY YOU GOT FITTER.

CrossFit, through the use of benchmark workouts, allows you to benchmark your level of fitness and gives you a 100% objective and numerical way to gauge your level of development and the results of your training. A benchmark workout is simply a standard workout—a workout everyone in the CrossFit community is familiar with. Alternatively, you can create your own benchmark workout that you use as a standard to gauge your own progress.

As a side note, CrossFit benchmark workouts are almost always given female names. One reason CrossFit is so revolutionary is that it allows everyone to speak a standardized language when it comes to fitness in much the same way poundage allow us to speak a common language about strength. If someone tells me they have a sub-six-minute Fran, I know a lot about their level of fitness and conditioning.

A good benchmark CrossFit workout for MILO readers is Linda:

10 reps of deadlift, bench press, clean
9 reps of deadlift, bench press, clean
8 reps of deadlift, bench press, clean
7 reps of deadlift, bench press, clean
6 reps of deadlift, bench press, clean
5 reps of deadlift, bench press, clean
4 reps of deadlift, bench press, clean
3 reps of deadlift, bench press, clean
2 reps of deadlift, bench press, clean
1 rep of deadlift, bench press, clean

Go for time (meaning as fast as possible), where the deadlift is 1.5 x bodyweight, the bench press is bodyweight, and the clean is 0.75 x bodyweight.

If you can do Linda faster than the last time you did it, you will not only be fitter all the way around, you will also have an objective metric relating to your fitness.

Another great workout that they used at the 2008 CrossFit Games is:

5 deadlifts at 275 lb.
10 burpees

Do 5 rounds for time.

It doesn't look like much, but it's tough! The burpees take a huge cardiovascular toll and fatigue your entire body. Each set of deadlifts gets heavier and more challenging and the cardiovascular demands increase with each round.

Burpees tax the cardio system as you fly through a cycle from vertical to horizontal to vertical . . . go fast enough and moving your bodyweight becomes a challenge.

All you do is grab the bar and stand up, but deadlifts work most of the muscles in your body, and when combined with burpees, it doesn't take a huge amount of weight to tax your fitness. This burpee–deadlift combo was part of the 2008 CrossFit Games (Aromas, California). Incidentally, the official wearing the hat at the right side of this photo is Kurtis Bowler (CoC#3–2000), one of the early CrossFitters and the owner of Rainier CrossFit, which in 2006 began sponsoring a drug-tested strongman contest to benefit Fragile-X research.

Randall J. Strossen photos.

As Dr. Ken E. Leistner said in the June 2009 issue of MILO ["Strength Skills: Lifting Hard and Heavy," Vol. 17. No. 1], "One has to *learn* how to train hard in order to train hard, in a highly intense manner, utilizing most if not all of one's momentary ability . . . " (italics mine). I believe CrossFit is an outstanding tool to learn to train hard, particularly in a way that is different from how most lifters train on a regular basis.

The suck
In CrossFit culture, it's all about "the suck." The suck is the feeling you get right around the middle of the workout when every cell in your body is screaming to stop. You're really uncomfortable, possibly scared you'll hurt yourself or have a heart attack, and you feel as if there's no way you can ever finish the workout. Feeling like this for brief periods—while keeping safe and sane in your training, of course—is the key to getting better at training hard. The more often you go here and emerge unscathed, the more you're able to dig deep when training gets hard and to push beyond your momentary limits. Many CrossFitters find that this ability to work through fear and discomfort carries over into other parts of their lives as well.

> THE SUCK IS THE FEELING YOU GET RIGHT AROUND THE MIDDLE OF THE WORKOUT WHEN EVERY CELL IN YOUR BODY IS SCREAMING TO STOP.

CrossFit workouts
Recently we did a workout at my gym that was based on a couplet of deadlifts and pull-ups. The deadlifts were light by powerlifting standards, just 225 lb. Pull-ups were the kipping style favored in CrossFit. The workout of the day (WOD) was as follows:

    21 deadlifts
    21 pull-ups
    15 deadlifts
    15 pull-ups
    9 deadlifts
    9 pull-ups

Go for time.

CrossFit workouts can always be tailored to fit and enhance training. The example above is a good one—two of my focus movements currently are deadlifts and pull-ups. Granted, the deadlifts were done light, but I did 45 reps in less than 10 minutes—and this was supersetted with pull-ups.

Let's look at what we got out of this classic CrossFit style workout:

- a lot of deadlift reps in a short time
- a lot of pull-up reps in a short time
- high systemic challenge
- massive stimulation of essentially all the musculature of the body (overall stimulation from the deadlift and isolated stimulation for the upper-body pulling structures from the pull-up)
- massive endocrine and nervous system stimulation
- high cardio–respiratory stimulation
- a darn fun and challenging workout!

One of the things that I love about CrossFit is that it gives a context within which you can really mix up workouts and bust out of a rut in training.

A workout like this will do just that for you.

Another format that my friend Merle McKenzie, owner of CrossFit USA in Berlin, Connecticut, uses is a compound barbell movement done in standard low-rep, rest-as-long-as-you-want fashion followed by a metabolic conditioning workout that may or may not include a barbell movement.

An example of this type of workout would be:

> max deadlift 5 x 5, then
>
> do 5 rounds for time:
> sprint 400 m
> 10 pull-ups
> 20 push-ups
> 30 sit-ups
> 40 air squats (no weight, below parallel, perfect form)

The above could be adjusted (scaled, in CrossFit terms) as follows for a heavy individual who doesn't run well and is limited in pull-ups due to heavy bodyweight:

> max deadlift 5 x 5, then
>
> jog 400 m, then
>
> do 5 rounds for time:
> 3 pull-ups
> 20 push-ups
> 30 sit-ups
> 40 air squats (no weight, below parallel, perfect form)
>
> jog (again) for 400 m

In this example, pull-ups were reduced from 10 to 3 per round, the sprint was changed to a jog, total rounds of jogging were reduced from 5 to 2, and jogging was removed from the timed portion of the workout.

Again, "for time" always means as fast as possible. In CrossFit gyms, everyone posts their time and other metrics on a big board to track progress and build a competitive environment.

Putting it all together

There are a number of different ways you can incorporate CrossFit-style work into your training. Since I assume you're already training hard and heavy with a barbell, I'll make the following suggestions:

- Do the CrossFit work on a rest day or substitute CrossFit for traditional cardio on your cardio days. CrossFit workouts are brief but very intense. Keep a close eye on your overall training volume and add the new training carefully, being aware of its effects on your recovery and progression.

- Try one of the CrossFit benchmark workouts and record your time. I'd suggest Linda, Helen, Angie, or Grace because they use movements and equipment you'll likely be familiar with. The deadlift–burpee workout above is also a good one.

- At a minimum, try about six CrossFit workouts over the course of the month. Always do a different workout and try to vary the content of the workouts as much as possible—don't choose the same type of workout for all of them. Mix it up and choose workouts that are as diverse as possible. Record your time and other metrics for all of them.

- Push yourself to do things you're not comfortable doing in the CrossFit sessions. If you hate running, emphasize workouts that require running. If you love doing barbell work, emphasize CrossFit workouts that use bodyweight calisthenic movements. The point is to train outside of your comfort zone at a very high intensity.

> CROSSFIT EXCELS AT EXPOSING HOLES IN YOUR CONDITIONING AND FORCING YOU TO BECOME A BETTER AND MORE COMPLETE ATHLETE.

Repeat the *same* benchmark workout you did at the beginning of the month and see what your time is—it should be faster, possibly a lot faster. At this point, you might also want to review your training log and see if there are any other improvements you can ascertain.

My final recommendation—other than to just do it—as it applies to experimenting with CrossFit is to start with the workouts I have here or those from the main site (www.crossfit.com). Do these at least until you have enough experience to put together a good CrossFit workout on your own. The main site posts a workout every night for the following day. Many Cross-Fitters started out doing the main site WOD in their garages.

The beauty of doing workouts from the CrossFit main website is that you never know what your workout is going to be and it will almost always include—or be entirely composed of—things you wouldn't do on your own or just plain aren't good at. CrossFit excels at exposing holes in your conditioning and forcing you to become a better and more complete athlete.

CrossFit works for improving the fitness of athletes in every discipline. Try it and see for yourself. M

References:

1. Greg Glassman, "Metabolic Conditioning" (*CrossFit Journal*, June 2003).
2. http://library.crossfit.com/free/pdf/CFJ-trial.pdf.

CALENDAR

Check out the Latest News at **www.ironmind.com**, the Strength World's News Source.

2010 NA Strongman, Inc.
For upcoming contests and information, visit www.nastrongman-inc.com or contact Willie and Dione Wessels, 314-770-9279, email: dione@americanstrongman.com.

2010 United States Armwrestling Association, Inc.
Apr 10	Jim Foster Memorial AW, Laurel, MT
Apr 10	2nd Annual Ronnie Coleman Classic AW, Mesquite, TX
Apr 16–17	2nd Annual Europa Show of Champions Pro-Am AW Championships, Orlando, FL
May 15–16	16th Annual USAA National Pro–Am AW Championships, Reno, NV
Jul 10	Oklahoma State Pro–Am AW Championships, Anadarko, OK
Jul 23–24	1st Annual Europa Battle of Champions AW, Hartford, CT
Aug 5–8	2010 USAF Unified National AW Championships, Billings, MT
Aug 13–14	17th Annual Europa Super Show Pro–Am AW Challenge, Dallas, TX

For more information, contact the USAA, 246 Custer Avenue, Billings, MT 59101; 406-248-4508 or 406-245-1560; www.usarmwrestling.com.

2010 United States All-Round W/L Assn.
For upcoming events and information, contact Bill Clark, 3906 Grace Ellen Drive, Columbia, MO 65202-1796. USAWA is a drug-free organization.

2010 Powerlifting
For scheduled events, check *Powerlifting USA* magazine. For subscription information, call 800-448-7693 or 805-482-2378.

2010 USA Weightlifting/IWF
Mar 5–7	Arnold WL Championships, Columbus, OH
Apr 2–11	European WL Championships, Minsk, Belarus
Apr 9–11	National Masters' WL Championships, Rego Park, NY
May 20–23	Pan-American WL Championships, Guatemala
Jun 11–13	National WL Championships, Peoria, IL
Jun 11–20	Junior World WL Championships, Sofia, Bulgaria
Sep 18–30	World WL Championships, Antalya, Turkey
Oct 3-14	Commonwealth Games, Delhi, India
Nov 12-27	Asian Games, Guangzhou, China

For more information on USA Weightlifting contests, please contact 719-866-4508 or www.usaweightlifting.org. For information about international competitions, please visit www.iwf.net.

2010 Highland Games
For schedules of competitions, please see the following websites:
. www.asgf.org
. www.saaa-net.org
. www.highlandnet.com
. www.nasgaweb.com

Taking on the
Steel Giant

The steel giant.
Photos courtesy of John Brookfield.

John Brookfield

Author of *Mastery of Hand Strength, Revised Edition, The Grip Master's Manual, Training with Cables for Strength,* and *Dexterity Ball Training for Hands*

I have been asked so many times how I prepare for pulling semi-trailer trucks for distance that I decided to share some of my training and strategy for the distance pulls. It is important to understand that pulling a semi-trailer truck for the distance of one mile is nothing like the short distance pulls of 30 yards or so—it is an entirely different animal and must be treated as such.

Looking back on the different one-mile pulls I have been involved in, I can say that each one had a different personality. I performed 3 or 4 one-mile pulls in the past with Steve Jeck and Kirk Nobles. Each time, we tried to push the envelope by pulling heavier loads or going up slight inclines. We also tried to avoid using any ropes for assistance. On a couple of the pulls we succeeded in not using the ropes and on a couple of occasions we had to bring them out in spots because of the incline we were facing. After 3 or 4 of these pulls, I decided to test our limits even more by pulling over several one-mile routes with the help of only one person, Jon Bruney. With only one other puller, you really have to make a commitment to yourself and your associate to stick with it no matter what.

Jon and I first pulled together in Manning, South Carolina, on a hot May afternoon with the temperature nearing 88 degrees and the humidity at almost 100 percent. Our load that day was over 20,000 lb. and our time was 1 hour 13 minutes. We never had to pull out the ropes even though we did have some inclines to deal with. This first one-mile pull with Jon was a great success. We pushed ourselves a bit more and on November 1 in Fairmont, North Carolina, we decided to go again for a one-mile pulling route. This time the steel giant was over 32,000 lb. The first three-quarters of the mile were pretty flat; however, the last 325 yards or so had a steady upgrade, which was visi-

> WITH ONLY ONE OTHER PULLER, YOU REALLY HAVE TO MAKE A COMMITMENT TO YOURSELF AND YOUR ASSOCIATE O STICK WITH IT NO MATTER WHAT.

ble even to the eye. The incline seemed to get steeper as we moved forward and we had to pretty much stay on all fours to keep the truck rolling. The truck driver said that the last 125 yards or so the truck was actually trying to roll backward. For the last 75 yards, Jon and I had to pull out the ropes to get any traction. We were able to pull the truck up the grade and finish the one-mile course in about 1 hour 30 minutes. It was a great experience, to say the least.

John Brookfield and Jon Bruney on a one-mile truck pull.

From there I had a goal to pull a truck a mile by myself sometime after my fiftieth birthday, so on the last Saturday in April 2009, I put the idea to the test and went up against a 24,000-lb. truck for the distance of one mile. I made sure that I had a flat stretch of ground for this record. After quite a bit of looking, I found the right spot for the pull. With more than a lot of effort and fortitude I was able to complete

> FIRST OF ALL, IT IS IMPORTANT TO UNDERSTAND THAT YOU MUST HAVE GREAT PHYSICAL AND MENTAL CONDITIONING.

the route in 1 hour 23 minutes. I was more than happy with the time and effort and also glad to get the job done before the extremely hot weather set in, as summer was approaching.

With all this said, it leads me back to the question I regularly receive from people about how I train and prepare for these records. First of all, it is important to understand that you must have great physical and mental conditioning. All the strength in the world won't help you accomplish this feat without great physical and mental conditioning. You may be surprised to learn that I don't do any traditional lifting at all. It may surprise you even more when I say I don't do any squats whatsoever, and I don't think they really help for an endurance event like this. Remember, you have to move forward, not upward, and success for distance pulling is based on movement, not lack thereof. My main training focus was four specific exercises, and I will share and briefly explain three of them in this article.

Weight carry

The first training method I used was the weight carry for distance up and down hills. I would usually walk for a mile, and sometimes two miles, carrying approximately 200 lb. on my shoulders. I quite often would use two 100-lb. weight vests from the MiR Vest company. I have a steep hill in front of my house that goes about 150 yards before it levels out. Going up the hill would greatly work my heart and lungs as well as my legs, core, back and traps. Going down the hill worked my stabilizers, which is crucial for core and leg strength. Because carrying weight is uncomfortable, it also develops mental discipline and perseverance. On occasion I would carry close to 300 lb. on my shoulders for a mile, which was really uncomfortable but got the job done.

Chain drag

Another training method I used was dragging heavy chains uphill behind my house in the sand. Chain dragging seems to work you much better than pulling a sled because of the length of the chains and the way that they pick up friction when they are dragged in the sand. I would pull several hundred pounds of chains for a mile and sometimes two miles. The combination of these two exercises was a great help and very applicable to truck pulling because both methods were based on forward movement—which is not the case in traditional lifting.

Hand-over-hand rope pull

The third exercise I would do is hand-over-hand rope pulling, which strengthened my upper body and hands in general and prepared me in case I got stuck on a hill and needed to increase traction. If you get stuck when using ropes and you have not been pulling on ropes, you are in danger of tearing your skin, which will hinder your pulling physically and mentally. Hand-over-hand rope pulling is great for upper-body strength—and for ensuring no weak links.

These drills, with their discomfort factor, are perfect for developing mental endurance. I also always train outside in the elements, which teaches you to persevere no matter what the weather and conditions bring. I hope this gives you some idea of the training and mindset I used to pull the trucks for distance and take on the steel giants.

Advancing Punching Power through Variable Method Complexes

Steven Helmicki

Author of *The Art of the Neck: Training for Distortion* and *Primordial Strength System*

Most men fight out of fear. The real fighters win without fear because their minds have led them to train everything right.

"The ability to fully and effectively utilize one's motor potential for achieving success is the essence of sport technical mastery. This ability is realized by means of a concrete system of movements and appropriate

criteria, the composition and organization of which are determined by the type of athletic activity."
—Verkhoshansky, *Fundamentals of Special Strength Training in Sport*

In other words, you will be more successful in your sport if you pick the right training methods.

Punching speed and power is determined by strength components much more complicated than raising the absolute strength output of the fighter. "Extraordinary development of absolute strength has a negative influence on speed," Verkhoshansky wrote in *Fundamentals of Special Strength Training in Sport*. One must keep in mind what we are measuring in fighters, why, and if we are using the right measures to begin with.

In *Managing the Training of Weightlifters*, Laputin and Oleshko wrote, "It has been established that the development of speed-strength is more effective the more speed exercises are included in training and the less [fewer] slow speed exercises are included in training."

This is one of the key components of how we build fighter training systems. Every time I see a numbers guy for a strength coach, I think, check yourself, your ego is involved. After absolute strength baselines are achieved at a level well below what is required for elite powerlifting or Olympic lifting, developing strength-speed, quickness, explosive power-endurance, speed-strength, elasticity, and reactive ability become paramount for success.

> ONE MUST KEEP IN MIND WHAT WE ARE MEASURING IN FIGHTERS, WHY, AND IF WE ARE USING THE RIGHT MEASURES TO BEGIN WITH.

Training according to the program described below more than adequately raises absolute strength to the desired levels and beyond. Thus, frequent maximum-effort training is not recommended because of 1) the risk-to-benefit ratio and 2) the decreasing speed that our experience has shown to be the result of maximum effort and progressive overload. We use seasoned trainees and fighters with decades of experience and high levels of absolute strength. Psychological inhibitors do play a role because of the fear of maximum bench presses (or other lifts) and seeing a lot of weight on the bar. The elasticity and improved reflexes gained from a variable method—alternating light to heavy, back and forth with weights in the strength-speed and speed-strength ranges—and maximum velocity is greater than with any other method I have seen to date.

Popular powerlifting methods are very effective for powerlifting, but the guy with the highest 1-rep max doesn't necessarily win the fight. Using these numbers in and of themselves as a gauge to punching output or fighting success is flawed. How tissue and power are acquired is critical to what is produced strengthwise in the athlete. The variable method, when used in longer, complex sequences, leads to advanced explosive power-endurance, elasticity, and reactive ability in a uniquely fast way. It had the most profound effect in trainees who were considered notoriously slow twitch.

If one accepts Verkhoshansky's assertion that "available data shows that the speed of the movement is enhanced to a large degree by the variable method [of] putting a shot 'fresh' from the muscular sensation obtained [first] from putting a lighter apparatus," the potential for adapting this to all movements and getting the same effect is very high. If it can be enhanced by repeating this order [e.g., going from a light shot to a standard shot] multiple times and the entire body is trained three times weekly, imagine what the gains in reactive, athletic muscle can be achieved.

With regard to overtraining, we have found with the variable method an enormous ability to recover quickly and effectively without layoffs. All who have used it report that they do not have the feelings of tiredness, soreness and lack of well-being they had experienced while taking max effort movements weekly or while on progressive overload. Much of the post-training lethargy and primary nervous system taxation seem to be associated with frequent max-effort exertion. Lifters may have the luxury of being sore and having output compromised frequently on a weekly, monthly, and yearly basis. However, this has a negative influence on the fighter physically, psychologically and emotionally. It also frequently interrupts teaching the primary motor skills. After all, fighters have to fight and they only get better by fighting and displaying their power development in that way. These athletes also report substantial improvements in testosterone levels without supplementation in comparison to when they were frequently taking maximums.

Steven Helmicki with contender winner Troy Ross after his sparring session with Lionel Thompson in Buffalo.
Courtesy of Steven Helmicki.

> AFTER ALL, FIGHTERS HAVE TO FIGHT AND THEY ONLY GET BETTER BY FIGHTING AND DISPLAYING THEIR POWER DEVELOPMENT IN THAT WAY.

"You are hitting the bag 50% harder," stated Jeremy Hall's boxing coach. "I'll tell you that I do get slightly winded by the end of the round, but then I am at full recovery very soon after rest and return to the next round with full wrestling and striking power in about a minute. This happens round after round," said Jeremy Hall, Buffalo Beast and MMA fighter. Jeremy gained 50% punching power and 14 lb. in 4 weeks while dropping 3% bodyfat from an already extremely tight 240 lb. Recovery capacity was quadrupled by means of typical conditioning (running and agility) mixed with powerlifting training. With the method presented here, two former USA Boxing Team members, Olympic Trials participants and current professionals Lionel Thompson and Excell Holmes have reported punching power that goes through the bag.

If you want to just hit the bag or be back-alley ready, or are the next wrestling, boxing or MMA star, train using the schedule below for four weeks and let us know if the heavy bag, a thug or your professional opponent is still holding its/his own with you. Train to win. Period. *Polskii Energii.*

Four-week program for an advanced trainee

Train 3 x per week and repeat the workouts with 15% reduction in rest time between complexes per week. Strive to improve and accelerate force continually. All other factors remain the same.

Day 1
12-kg kettlebell 6" box jumps x 2
16-kg kettlebells 6" box jumps x 2
Below parallel box squat 100-lb. barbell x 2
Repeat this cycle x 4 without stopping

1 minute rest/hydration

Landmine* one-arm press empty bar x 2
Landmine press 25 lb. x 2
Landmine press 50 lb. x 2
Repeat this cycle x 4 without stopping

1 minute rest/hydration

Chins bodyweight x 2
Chins 25 lb. x 2
Repeat this cycle x 5 without stopping

1 minute rest/hydration

Kettlebell high pulls 12 kg x 2; 24 kg x 2
Repeat x 3 without stopping

1 minute rest/hydration

Kettlebell curls 4 kg x 4; 8 kg x 4
Repeat x 4 without stopping

1 minute rest/hydration

Average band pushdown x 2; strong band pushdown x 2
Repeat x 4 without stopping

1 minute rest/hydration

Kettlebell swings 12 kg x 3; 24 kg x 3
Repeat x 4 without stopping

Neck harness flexion/extension 6 kg x 3; 12 kg x 3
Repeat this cycle x 4 without stopping

Trainer Captains of Crush Gripper x 3;
No. 1 CoC Gripper x 3
Repeat x 3 without stopping

*Substitute dumbbells or a barbell if you do not have access to the Sorinex Landmine

Day 2
Trap bar deadlift 95 lb. x 2; 190 lb. x 2
Repeat x 4 without stopping

1 minute rest/hydration

Kettlebell cleans and presses 12 kg x 2; 24 kg x 2
Repeat x 3 without stopping

1 minute rest/hydration

Kettlebell shrugs 24 kg x 5; 48 kg x 5
Repeat x 4 without stopping

1 minute rest/hydration

Straight bar curl 45 lb. x 3; 90 lb. x 3
Repeat x 4 without stopping

1 minute rest/hydration

Close grip bench 45 lb. x 3; 90 lb. x 3
Repeat x 5 without stopping

1 minute rest/hydration

Landmine twist empty bar x 3; 25 lb. x 3; 50 lb. x 3
Repeat x 2 without stopping

1 minute rest/hydration

Neck harness 16 kg x 3 reps x 5 sets, 4 seconds rest between sets

Day 3
Kettlebell trampoline jumps 4 kg x 2; 8 kg x 2
Repeat this cycle x 4 without stopping

1 minute rest/hydration

Shoulder width free squat 95 lb. x 2; 185 lb. x 2
Repeat x 4 without stopping

1 minute rest/hydration

Two sprint step starts light band x 2; average band x 2 (band around waist, start to sprint taking two steps against resistance)
Repeat x 3 without stopping

1 minute rest/hydration

Nautilus/alternative kettlebell pullover 50 lb. x 3; 100 lb. x 3
Repeat x 3 without stopping

1 minute rest/hydration

Kettlebell bench 12 kg x 4; 24 kg x 4
Repeat x 3 without stopping

1 minute rest/hydration

Hise shrugs 135 lb. x 4; 270 lb. x 4
Repeat x 4 without stopping

1 minute rest/hydration

Face pulls monster mini-band x 3; light band x 3
Repeat x 4 without stopping

1 minute rest/hydration

Kettlebell curls 4 kg x 2; 8 kg x 2; 12 kg x 2
Repeat x 3 without stopping

1 minute rest/hydration

Kettlebell swings 8 kg x 2; 16 kg x 2; 32 kg x 2
Repeat x 3 without stopping

1 minute rest/hydration

Nautilus 4-way neck: 2 plates x 3; 4 plates x 3
Repeat x 3 without stopping

Getting the Body Ripped and Toned in a Fast and Healthy Way

Steve Justa

Author of *Rock Iron Steel: The Book of Strength*

Getting the body ripped and toned is something I have got to talk about. I've got 30 years of training under my belt and I've experimented and done almost all kinds of training that you could imagine. I've experimented on myself over and over again, and I want to tell MILO readers what I've learned about getting your body in super good shape.

There are more than 650 muscles in the body, and an old-time strongman named Arthur Saxon back in 1900 wrote that fat cannot exist on a thoroughly exercised muscle for very long. Saxon was, and still is, one of the strongest and most well-conditioned strength athletes the world has ever known. He weighed 200 lb. and could put a 370-lb. barbell above his head with one arm. He was walking with "well over a ton" behind his neck on his shoulders at 200-lb. bodyweight. I'll bet you there's nobody alive in the world today who could do that. He never took drugs or steroids—way back in 1900 they didn't even have that kind of stuff.

I myself have found what Saxon says about muscles and fat to be true. If you go through and do all different kinds of lifts and you try to directly hit all your muscles from all different angles and directions, your physical body will shed excess weight very quickly. When you hit different muscles, you activate different nerves, and these nerves make the muscles start working, which in turn starts getting the muscles more powerful, creating more endurance and stamina and burning off the fat. What really bothers me is when you can go to any gym in the country and see people training on treadmills or bicycles. Most people will train for an hour, which is great. But the mistake most of them make is that they do only one or two different disciplines for that whole hour—and they do this day after day and wonder why it's taking so long to get in really good shape. It's very simple: they are not working enough different muscles. Yes, they are working hard, but not smart.

> IT'S VERY SIMPLE: THEY ARE NOT WORKING ENOUGH DIFFERENT MUSCLES. YES, THEY ARE WORKING HARD, BUT NOT SMART.

If you're going to train to get ripped, you have to work all your muscles, not just a few. Take it from me—or Saxon—I know what I'm talking about. Saxon said when you train, you should do every lift you can think of: one-arm lifts, two-arm lifts, quarter-overload movements off the floor, holds for time, walking, supporting, pressing, and pulling. Try to pull in and work thoroughly every different scrap of muscle you can think of. Do things on your toes and flat-footed; do lifts with

> Swim, play basketball, work in your garden—it doesn't matter what you do, just do any different thing you can think of.

your legs in different stances, standing and kneeling; do things with your waist bent or twisted. Try to work every joint in a 360-degree angle, including your waist. Do holds for time, pull things sideways with your waist straight and also bent over. Do shoulder carries. Do every different possible thing you can think of. Ride a bike, run, walk, use weight vests. Do pull-ups, curls, isometrics, one-hand lifts, overhead lifts, rows, squats, half squats, quarter squats, full squats. Do both partial movements and full movements, and holds for time. Swim, play basketball, work in your garden—it doesn't matter what you do, just do any different thing you can think of. There are a thousand different things you can do: stair climbing, carrying objects, walking on the sides of ditches, boxing a wall, kicking things, punching, wrestling someone.

The more different muscles you work and hit directly and toughly, the quicker and faster you will rip up into tremendous shape. At the same time, you are gaining muscle coordination, which gives you the ability to be a super athlete. You'll feel so much better because when you activate all those different nerves, you're pushing the poisons out of those unused muscles. It really does make good sense.

When you're out to get ripped, you should be doing something—and a lot of different things—every day, for at least two hours a day. You don't have to do it all at once; do a little here and a little there, off and on if you want to—it all adds up in the end. If you're at work, start tensing different muscles and hold them from time to time. Anything and everything you do will pay off for you. If you're going to train and put all that time in, you might as well get the most out of it. Work all those twisting muscles in your waist, legs, arms, shoulders, feet, and ankles. Do as many different things as you can possibly think of—use your imagination. This is how you get ripped. A month of this and you'll be stunned at the results you get, I'll guarantee it.

Another good tip is whatever you do, try not to tire out yourself or your muscles too much. What I mean is, try to always keep your oxygen level high. Stop each exercise long before failure or oxygen loss creeps in. Stop each exercise while you feel fresh, and then rest and do it again and again. Then go to something else. This way you are putting a constant drain on and using the muscles without overly tiring them. This regulated effort keeps up your oxygen level in the muscle, stops lactic acid from forming, and burns more fat. You'll feel fresher and will be able to work out longer and keep from getting sore. Then, of course, the better shape you get into, the longer and harder you can push all your exercises without becoming tired. It just makes sense and it is Mother Nature's way of doing things.

Keep all of this in mind and as long as you don't eat tons of food every day, I will practically guarantee you you'll get ripped—quicker than you imagined.

2009 World Weightlifting Championships: Lift the Limit

Jim Schmitz

U.S. Olympic Team Weightlifting Coach 1980, 1988, & 1992

"Lift the limit" was the motto of the 2009 World Weightlifting Championships held in Goyang City, Korea, 20–29 November. Goyang City is the hometown of Jang Mi-ran, Korea's Olympic and world champion and world-record holder in the women's +75-kg weight class. Located just north of Seoul, *Newsweek* magazine designated Goyang City as one of the ten most dynamic cities in the world. I don't quite know what they meant by that, but it is certainly a city under construction.

The competition was staged at the Kintex Convention Center, which is gigantic. The weightlifting competition was held in one of the five convention center halls, with seating for about two thousand people. Also in this hall were the warm-up room, which held 16 platforms; a training hall with 50 platforms; and the offices for the press, IWF, and competition management. I think the Kintex Convention Center is bigger than the Georgia Convention Center where, during the 1996 Olympics, weightlifting plus five other sports were held. The sponsors for these Worlds were the City of Goyang, the Korean Weightlifting Federation, and their many supporters. They really did an outstanding job of organizing and running this World Championships—every detail was covered and no expense spared; for example, Uesaka barbells custom printed with "Goyang" on each plate were used.

Of the competitors, 196 men from 57 countries and 133 women from 38 countries took to the platform, for a total of 329 athletes. It's normal for there to be a smaller turnout the year after the Olympics. At the Worlds in 2005 there were 112 women and 169 men for a 281 total; in 2001 there were 114 women and 152 men for a

266 total; and in 1997, with 9 weight classes for women and 10 for men, there were 143 women and 190 men for 333 total. Also, there were other Asian events going on around this time—the East Asian Games and the Southeast Asian Games were being held in December. The Chinese lifters all said they hadn't recovered from the Chinese National Games, which is a really big deal for them and were held just one month earlier. Bulgaria was not there due to their suspension for drug positives. Greece also wasn't there, but I'm not sure of the reason. Unfortunately, many of the stars from the Beijing Olympics were either injured or just not in shape and therefore not there.

56-kg class
The men's 56-kg class had two Chinese juniors, 18-year-old Olympic champion Long Qingquan (he turned 19 on December 3) and Wu Jingbiao (who turned 20 January 10), lifting and they pretty much owned the class. Missing was Vietnam's Olympic silver medalist, Hoang Anh Tuan and the entire Vietnamese team, who I was told were preparing for the Southeast Asian Games.

Wu and Long went lift for lift in the snatch, with Wu making 131 kg on his third attempt and Long missing 132 kg on his third. In the clean and jerk it was all Long—Wu could only make his opener with 155 kg. Long secured the gold with his first clean and jerk of 156 kg and then did a very strong 162 kg. He then called for a world record 169 kg (triple bodyweight); he cleaned it strong and jerked it, but his right arm buckled and he couldn't hold it—no lift. He had made this weight at the Chinese National Games, but it didn't count as a world record as world records can be set only in IWF-designated competitions.

Long really enjoyed his lifting—he was smiling, laughing, and having a good time. Of course, maybe you would too if at 17 years old you were an Olympic champion and at 18 a world champion.

Cuba's Sergio Alvarez came from fifth place in the snatch to win bronze medals in the clean and jerk and total.

62-kg class
The 62s also had two Chinese lifters entered: Ding Jianjun, a junior, and Yang Fan. They would take first and second, respectively, in the snatch, with lifts of 146 and 144 kg. The clean and jerk brought some surprises and upsets. Indonesia's Eko Irawan, a junior, made three very strong clean and jerks with 166, 171, and 175 for the gold in the clean and jerk and the silver in the total, beating Yang by 1 kg. Irawan and his coach, Enda Nasution (seventh in the 60-kg class at the 1984 Olympics), argued over the final clean and jerk weight. Irawan wanted 178 kg for a junior world record—and this was his last chance—but the coach wanted 175 for the gold medal. The coach won the argument and Irawan made a very strong 175 for the gold in the clean and jerk and the silver in the total.

> Long really enjoyed his lifting—he was smiling, laughing, and having a good time.

> Irawan and his coach, Enda Nasution (seventh in the 60-kg class at the 1984 Olympics), argued over the final clean and jerk weight.

Taipei's Yang Sheng-Hsiung had clean and jerked 170 in the B session and that held up for the silver medal. This class had an exciting and close finish: Ding totaled 316 kg, Irawan 315 kg, and Yang 314 kg.

69-kg class

China's Liao Hui owned the 69-kg class, winning three gold medals pretty much unchallenged. After he won the gold in the snatch with his second attempt with 160 kg, he tried the world record 166, which he had up but then lost behind him. Liao's elbow touched his knee on his first attempt clean and jerk with 186; he then made it with no problem and passed on his third attempt.

There was a good battle for second place. Romania's Ninel Miculescu made all his snatches, beating Armenia's Arakel Mirzoyan 155 kg to 154. In the clean and jerk, Korea's Kim Sun-Bae made 181 to beat Indonesia's Triyatno and Mirzoyan, who had done 180 in the clean and jerk. Mirzoyan's 154 snatch and 180 clean and jerk held up for second place in the total, with Triyatno in third with 150 and 180. Miculescu couldn't keep up in the clean and jerk and was only able to make his opener of 173 kg.

This was a very exciting session for second place, and it's very interesting to note that Arakel Mirzoyan is the son of Oksen Mirzoyan, Armenia's 1988 Olympic champion and 1983 world champion in the 56-kg class. Oksen was coaching Arakel and was very proud and happy.

77-kg class

There were two Chinese in the 77-kg class, Lu Xiaojun and Su Dajin, and Armenia's Tigran Martirosyan to take on Korea's Olympic champion, Sa Jae-Hyouk. Lu made three fantastic snatches, 165, 170, and the world record 174 kg for the gold, while Martirosyan made 170 for the silver, and Su did 165 for the bronze medal. Sa made only his opener with 160, which left him in fifth place—even with his big clean and jerk ability he was in trouble.

In the clean and jerk, Lu and Su had successful openers with 200 kg. Martirosyan had an elbow touch on his opener with 200, but he made it with no problem on his second attempt. Lu then successfully made 204 kg for the world record total and a commanding lead that no one could challenge, so they were just going for medals in the clean and jerk and for second place. Sa opened with a hard but good 205, which proved to be too much for Su and Martirosyan. Lu then called for 211 kg for the world record and missed the clean. Sa took 212 for his second attempt, cleaned it, but missed the jerk. Sa took the world-record 212 again on his third attempt, made a really gut-straining clean, and jerked it—but it was turned down 2 to 1. I thought it was good, but I am a fan of big clean and jerks and think if someone can press out a world-record jerk, that is one strong lifter and he deserves the lift—but rules are rules and they must be followed. Sa ended up getting fourth place on bodyweight to Su. It was interesting that Lu and Su are squat jerkers, and Martirosyan is a power jerker—but Sa is a splitter!

85-kg class

Olympic 85-kg champion Lu Yong was entered, but not Belarus's world cham-

> SA TOOK THE WORLD-RECORD 212 AGAIN ON HIS THIRD ATTEMPT, MADE A REALLY GUT-STRAINING CLEAN, AND JERKED IT— BUT IT WAS TURNED DOWN 2 TO 1.

With a silver medal and two golds in his pocket, Long Quingguan (China) attacked 169 kg, going for the junior and senior world records in the jerk, as well as the junior world record in the total. He cleaned the weight, but missed the jerk.

All photos by Randall J. Strossen

Hitting this 146-kg snatch put China's Ding Jianjun in the driver's seat— it gave him the gold medal in the snatch and a 6-kg lead going into the clean and jerk.

© RANDALL J. STROSSEN, PH.D.

Eurosport television anchor David Goldstrom said, "Randy, I told you: no photos of me." Strossen, who as the expert commentator for Eurosport was backing up Goldstrom, said, "It's for your mother, David."

MILO publisher Randall Strossen couldn't shake a back pain so he enlisted the help of the German team's ace physiotherapist Damiano Belvedere, who diagnosed the program as being a cramp—which he proceeded to grind at full strength, knuckles forward. "How do you feel now?" Damiano asked. "Much better since you stopped," Strossen said. Damiano smiled, "They call me 'The Pain Man.'"

After winning the snatch by 5 kg, Liao Hui (China) was pretty casual about the clean and jerk. He missed the jerk on his 186-kg opener, seemed completely unfazed by it, and repeated with the weight for a solid success on his second attempt. He then called it a night, leaving with three gold medals and a 12-kg winning margin.

China's Lu Xiaojun outdueled Armenia's Tigran Martirosyan for top honors, starting things off by sticking this 174-kg snatch—good for a world record, the gold medal, and a 4-kg lead over his rival. In the jerk, Lu Xiaojun also beat Martirosyan by 4 kg.

The man with the golden knife—this is Marek Krochmalski, M.D., the surgeon who operated on Mariusz Pudzianowski's knee and, according to the good doctor, is Mariusz's first choice when it's time to bring a scalpel into play. At the Worlds, among other things, Dr. Krochmalski was putting his new Nikon D-300 to good use.

Iranian super heavyweight Saeed Ali-Hosseini snatched this 200 kg with commanding ease in the training hall days before he was to have competed. Nicu Vlad (Romania), who knows a thing or two about snatching big weights, was also watching and he commented on how strong Ali-Hosseini looked on the lift.

Lyn Jones might look as if he's cutting in, but he's actually offering a steadying hand as Yurik Sarkisian dances on the back of Australian superheavyweight Corran Hocking.

Lu Yong (China) splits, driving himself under 211 kg on his third-attempt jerk. He missed the lift, but took home two golds and a silver in the 85-kg category.

The latest Kazakh wonder, Vladimir Sedov showed why even if your name is Ilya Ilin, you'd better keep your foot on the gas and an eye on the rearview mirror because coach Alexei Ni seems to have a formula for producing top lifters on a regular basis. Sedov posted a 402-kg total, a big number for anyone, but considering his youth and relative inexperience, not to mention his improvement since the 2008 Olympics, this was a pretty huge performance.

Marcin Dolega (Poland) has crossed swords with Dmitri Lapikov (Russia) before and once again, there was big pressure on the Pole to pull out a tough clean and jerk. This 226 kg fit the bill—he missed it on his second attempt but made it when he repeated, and as a result he left Korea as the 105-kg world champion.

An Yong-Kwon (Korea) only made one snatch, but he ran through three good clean and jerks, including this last attempt of the championships, 247 kg . . . the lift he needed and the lift he made to win the super heavyweight title.

John Coffee, who Randall Strossen calls the Lost Prophet of Weightlifting, made the trip to Korea as the personal coach of Kelly Rexroad, who went six for six.

69-kg Sarah Bertram (USA) went five for six and hit this PR snatch of 89 kg.

48-kg Kelley Rexroad (USA) nailed this 88-kg jerk, for a perfect day.

Jim Schmitz looks serious while studying the scoreboard in between videoing and taking photos. Jim also helped to coach Sarah Bertram for Tom Hirtz, who had to stay home in Oregon, honoring his other commitments.

pion and world record holder Andrei Rybakou. We were told he was recovering from a back injury and not in shape for the Worlds. Siarhei Lahun (Belarus) made all three snatches—163, 168, and 171 kg—for the bronze. Tigran Martirosyan of Armenia (no relation to the 77-kg lifter, they just have same name, which is common in Armenia) could only make his opener with 172 for the silver. Lu did 170 and 175 before missing 177 and won the gold. Sixth place in the snatch was 170 kg—this was a close and exciting snatch competition.

Lahun opened his clean and jerks with 200 kg, and then did 205 followed by another strong success with 209—he went six for six with a nice 380-kg total. Lu opened with 206 and then took 208 to secure the victory; he cleaned 211, but missed the jerk. Martirosyan dropped out of the competition due to an injury; however, his countryman Gervorik Poghosyan snatched 166 and clean and jerked 201 and 208 for the clean and jerk bronze. Kazakhstan's Vladimir Kuznetsov was fifth in the snatch with 170 and fourth in the clean and jerk with 206 for 376 kg and third place in the total.

Five different lifters won medals! Lu's victory completed China's sweep of the 56-, 62-, 69-, 77-, and 85-kg classes—and China said they weren't in top shape because they just had their Chinese National Games four weeks earlier!

94-kg class

The 94s were missing Kazakhstan's Olympic champion Ilya Ilin, who was not there also because of a back injury and not being in top shape. However, the day before, we were told that 21-year-old Vladimir Sedov, who was fourth in Beijing in the 85s with a 380-kg total, would impress us—and he did. He made three beautiful snatches with 177, 182, and 185 for the gold. Ukraine's Artem Ivanov, who lifted in the B group, got the silver with his 180 kg; however, he only cleaned and jerked 200 so he ended up in seventh place overall. Korea's Kim Min-Jae made 175 and 178 for the bronze.

There was a lot of strategy going on in the clean and jerk. Sedov opened with 210 kg; another Korean, Kim Seon-Jong, who was heavier, opened with 211; then Sedov made 217, followed by Kim Seon-Jong's 218. From there they kept jumping—220, 221, 222, 223—until finally Sedov had used up all his weight changes and took 225, but he couldn't clean it. Kim Seon-Jong had to take 226, but also couldn't clean it. Kim Seon-Jong had bluffed Sedov out of the gold in the clean and jerk.

This class had six men win medals: Sedov, Nizami Pashayev (Azerbaijan), and Kim Min-Jae in the total; Sedov, Ivanov, and Kim Min-Jae in the snatch; and Kim Seon-Jong, Sedov, and Valeriu Calancea (Romania) in the clean and jerk. Sedov looked as if he could lift more weight, so hopefully Ilin and Poland's Szymon Kolecki, who was also missing due to injuries, will meet next year in Antalya, Turkey to see who will be the new king of the 94s.

105-kg class

In the 105s, Andrei Aramnau, Belarus's Olympic champion, world champion, and junior and senior world record holder, was entered, and we were really looking forward to seeing him lift, but he had pulled a thigh muscle in training just a few days before. The contest was going to be between Poland's Marcin Dolega and Russia's Dmitry Lapikov (who beat Dolega on bodyweight for the bronze medal in Beijing), both totaling 420 kg. Lapikov opened with 186, followed by Dolega missing 191 miserably. I thought, oh boy, here we go again. Lapikov made the 191 easily enough, followed by Dolega making it as well. Lapikov then had another fine success with 194. Dolega needed 195 as he was heavier, and he made another hard, but successful lift.

> LU'S VICTORY COMPLETED CHINA'S SWEEP OF THE 56-, 62-, 69-, 77-, AND 85-KG CLASSES—AND CHINA SAID THEY WEREN'T IN TOP SHAPE . . .

> LAPIKOV OPENED WITH 186, FOLLOWED BY DOLEGA MISSING 191 MISERABLY.

Dolega opened his clean and jerks with 221 kg. Lapikov followed with 222, tying Dolega in the total but putting himself ahead on bodyweight. Dolega jumped to 226 and got pinned in the clean (I thought he took too big of a jump and had just cost himself the championships), but he came back and made a gutsy lift—all his lifts looked heavy, but he was strong and determined. Lapikov needed 227, which he called for, but he let the time run out. He then took it on his third attempt and cleaned it, but there was no way on the jerk. At the press conference he said he injured his thigh and that's why he let the time run out on his second attempt—so he could rest and give it his all-out effort on the third attempt, but he just couldn't push off his thigh for the jerk.

> DR. KROCHMALSKI SAID THEY USED STEM CELLS FROM DOLEGA'S OWN BLOOD . . . BUT FELT THIS COULD BE A BIG BREAKTHROUGH.

The final was three gold medals for Dolega, three silver medals for Lapikov, and three bronze medals for Georgia's Albert Kuzilov, with 187 and 221 for 408 kg. Also, at the press conference the Polish team doctor, Dr. Marek Krochmalski, said that Dolega had a new type of knee surgery in March 2009. They injected stem cells into his knees to repair his cartilage and his results here proved that it worked. Dr. Krochmalski said they used stem cells from Dolega's own blood—he didn't know if this had been done on knees before, but felt this could be a big breakthrough.

+105-kg class
And finally the last session was the +105s, the super heavyweights. Once again there was some disappointment as the new Iranian sensation, 21-year-old Saeid Ali-Hosseini, holder of all the junior world records (206, 245, and 451 kg), withdrew from the competition due to an injury to his arm (I didn't hear any specifics). Several people, including MILO publisher Randall Strossen, had seen Saeid snatch 200 and clean and jerk 240 just a few days before in the training hall. Everyone knew going in that Olympic champion Matthias Steiner wasn't entered; his coach Frank Mantek had announced it a couple of weeks before the Worlds, saying that due to a surgery in the spring and all the celebrations and recognitions for his winning the Olympics, Mathias just wasn't able to get into top shape.

I thought the battle would be between Ukraine's Artem Udachyn and Ihor Shymechko and Latvia's Viktors Scerbatihs. Korea's An Yong-Kwon had an impressive 450-kg total listed on the start list, but we hadn't seen him since 2004, where he placed eighth with a 427.5 total, so I didn't know what to expect. The starting weight for the big guys was 195 kg and Scerbatihs and Udachyn made it very easily. Shymechko opened with a very strong 197. An missed his opener with 198 and then made it, but it didn't look strong. Scerbatihs and Udachyn both missed 200 kg on their second, Scerbatihs missed it on his third, and Udachyn made it very well. Shymechko made another very nice snatch with 202 kg. An called for 206, but it wasn't close. Shymechko tried 206 as well, but to no avail. Scerbatihs dropped out—I don't know if he was injured or what.

> HE MADE IT WITH ROOM TO SPARE AND FOR THE FIRST TIME AN ASIAN WAS THE SUPER HEAVYWEIGHT WORLD CHAMPION . . .

In the clean and jerk, Shymechko missed his opener with 223 kg and jumped to 225 and made it with no problem, but his third attempt with 230 was just too heavy. A battle began between Udachyn and An. Udachyn opened with 231 and An opened with a very strong 233. Egypt's Mohamed Attiaa Ehssan clean and jerked 234, which was passed by the referees but overturned by the jury, costing him a medal—a real shame; again, I thought it was a good lift. Udachyn took and made 238; An, who is lighter, made 240, again with no problem—this was getting exciting! Udachyn took another 7-kg increase to 245, which he struggled to make, but he was tough and hung in there for three white lights. An needed 247 for the gold and the championships.

He made it with room to spare and for the first time an Asian was the super heavyweight world champion—a fantastic finish for the Worlds and for the Koreans. It's another first for Korea that it won both the women's and men's super heavyweight divisions. To me, there is nothing better than when the last lift of the World Championships or the Olympics determines the winner!

USA had nine men competing here, seven of whom placed. Aaron Adams placed 28th in the 62-kg class with 107 and 140 kg. Henry Brower did 127 and 160 for 12th place in the 69s, and Caleb Williams did 124 and 151 for 18th place in the same class. In the 85s, Kendrick Farris did 154 and 191 for 12th place, and Matt Bruce did 147 and 191 for 13th place. Cody Gibbs went six for six, ending with a PR of 167 and 190 for 14th place in the 105s. In the +105s, Patrick Judge also went six for six, reaching several PRs and finishing with 171 and 217 for 388 kg and our highest placing of 9th. Lance Frye was selected for the team but had transportation problems and didn't make the trip.

In the women's team competition China was first with 514 points, Korea second with 429, Turkey third with 408, Russia fourth with 398, Kazakhstan fifth with 385 and only six lifters competing, and Mexico sixth with 273; USA was fifteenth with 195 points. Kazakhstan had three women world champions and one male world champion—pretty impressive and a great testament to their longtime coach Alexei Ni, who is assisted by Enver Turkileri (the famous coach of Naim Suleymanoglu). Jang Mi-ran was selected as the outstanding woman lifter even though Svetlana Podobedova had the higher Sinclair point rating of 329.8797 to Jang's 324.1124. Jang was selected by the Eleiko–IWF Press Commission, and I certainly had no argument with that, as I now feel Jang is the greatest woman weightlifter of all time. Just look up her performances from 2003 until now and you'll see what I mean.

In the men's team competition, China was first with 623 points, Korea second with 503, Russia third with 392, Azerbaijan fourth with 355, Cuba fifth with 353, Ukraine sixth with 332, and USA tenth with 225 points. It's interesting to note that the great Bulgarian Olympic and world champion Yanko Rusev is now the coach of the

Azerbaijan team, and Nizami Pashayev (second in the 94s) says he is inspired and enthused by Rusev. Lu Xiaojun, who set two world records, was the outstanding male lifter with 476.2904 Sinclair points—well ahead of the rest of the competition and also selected by the Eleiko-IWF Press Commission.

The 2010 World Weightlifting Championships will be held in Antalya, Turkey, from 18-30 September 2010. The World Weightlifting Championships is the greatest weightlifting show on Earth even when it is considered an off year. The 2009 World's didn't count toward Olympic qualifying slots. Slots for the number of lifters a country can have in the Olympics are determined by team placings at the World Championships. The 2010 Worlds in Antalya and 2011 in Paris will count, so the competition will be getting tougher and fiercer as all the countries will definitely bring their big guns to earn slots for London in 2012. Who from the 2009 Worlds in Korea will be the stars and champions of 2010, 2011, and the 2012 Olympics? M

2009 World Weightlifting Championships – Final Results Men's A Session (Top 8)
Goyang City, South Korea, 20-29 November 2009

Rank	Name	Nat	BW	Snatch	C&J	Total
56-kg class						
1	LONG Qingquan	CHN	55.43	130	162	292
2	WU Jingbiao	CHN	56.00	131	155	286
3	ALVAREZ Sergio	CUB	55.85	120	154	274
4	SETIADI Jadi	INA	55.44	123	150	273
5	EL MAOUI Khalil	TUN	55.78	125	146	271
6	MAKAROV Ruslan	UZB	55.71	117	144	261
7	YANG Chin-yi	TPE	55.86	115	145	260
8	YAMADA Masaharu	JPN	55.92	109	150	259
62-kg class						
1	DING Jianjun	CHN	61.85	146	170	316
2	IRAWAN Eko Yuli	INA	61.68	140	175	315
3	YANG Fan	CHN	61.65	144	170	314
4	FIGUEROA Mosquera O.	COL	61.72	139	168	307
5	YANG Sheng-hsiung	TPE	61.44	130	170	300
6	SULEYMANOV Zulfugar	AZE	61.83	133	165	298
7	RUIZ Lazaro	CUB	60.48	135	161	296
8	BEHROUZI Sajad	IRI	61.64	135	161	296
69-kg class						
1	LIAO Hui	CHN	68.92	160	186	346
2	MIRZOYAN Arakel	ARM	68.61	154	180	334
3	TRIYATNO	INA	68.16	150	180	330
4	MICULESCU Ninel	ROU	68.54	155	173	328
5	KIM Sun-Bae	KOR	68.60	142	181	323
6	ROQUE Bredni	CUB	68.48	143	175	318
7	ABDEL TAWWAB M.	EGY	68.41	141	172	313
8	MENDIBAEV Bakhram	UZB	68.88	140	173	313
77-kg class						
1	LU Xiaojun	CHN	76.35	174*	204	378*
2	MARTIROSYAN Tigran G.	ARM	76.44	170	200	370
3	SU Dajin	CHN	76.34	165	200	365
4	SA Jae-Hyouk	KOR	76.54	160	205	365
5	CAMBAR Ivan	CUB	76.30	160	196	356
6	YEHIA Tarek	EGY	76.75	156	197	353
7	QERIMAJ Erkand	ALB	76.63	156	193	349
8	KIM Kwang-Hoon	KOR	76.49	153	193	346
85-kg class						
1	LU Yong	CHN	84.68	175	208	383
2	LAHUN Siarhei	BLR	83.90	171	209	380
3	KUZNETSOV Vladimir	KAZ	83.93	170	206	376
4	POGHOSYAN Gevorik	ARM	84.85	166	208	374
5	ZAIROV Intiqam	AZE	84.53	170	203	373
6	ZIELINSKI Adrian	POL	84.94	171	201	372
7	HERNANDEZ Yoelmis	CUB	83.93	162	205	367
8	KHAMATSHIN Roman	RUS	84.62	161	200	361
94-kg class						
1	SEDOV Vladimir	KAZ	92.23	185	217	402
2	PASHAYEV Nizami	AZE	93.75	177	210	387
3	KIM Min-Jae	KOR	93.86	178	206	384
4	KIM Seon-Jong	KOR	92.89	165	218	383
5	DEMANOV Andrey	RUS	93.72	171	210	381
6	FUTULLAYEV Rovshan	AZE	92.99	170	210	380
7	IVANOV Artem	UKR	93.64	180	200	380
8	BRATAN Evgheni	MDA	93.90	174	203	377
105-kg class						
1	DOLEGA Marcin	POL	104.95	195	226	421
2	LAPIKOV Dmitry	RUS	104.45	194	222	416
3	KUZILOV Albert	GEO	104.65	187	221	408
4	KONSTANTINOV Roman	RUS	101.31	180	220	400
5	TOROKHTIY Oleksiy	UKR	104.31	180	215	395
6	KIM Wha-Seung	KOR	104.95	182	210	392
7	DOLEGA Robert	POL	104.95	175	216	391
8	MACHAVARIANI Gia	GEO	104.09	180	210	390
+105-kg class						
1	AN Yong-Kwon	KOR	142.23	198	247	445
2	UDACHYN Artem	UKR	158.90	200	245	445
3	SHYMECHKO Ihor	UKR	133.82	202	225	427
4	MOHAMED Abdel R.	EGY	122.15	185	230	415
5	EHSSAN ATTIAA M.	EGY	149.38	185	230	415
6	VELAGIC Almir	GER	133.72	185	228	413
7	KOZLOV Andrey	RUS	145.75	180	231	411
8	ORSAG Jiri	CZE	122.95	170	218	388

*=WR

Stanless Steel:
Man of Steel

Mike Corlett

November, 2009, Los Angeles, California. I walked onto the street in front of the Downtown Independent movie theater, having just watched director Zach Levy's first film, a documentary called *Strongman*. A few feet away, the director was speaking to a small group of theater patrons. The star of the film, standing at the edge of the group, politely chatted and answered any and all questions they had of him. Seeing me, he grinned and discreetly motioned me over. "Mike," he said in a cheerful half whisper, "the way you mashed that IronMind 2.5 earlier today, I can tell that certification on the No. 3 is coming real soon!" Stanless Steel—performing strongman, Captain of Crush, small-business owner, and now the subject of a full-length film—is excited for this 55-year-old accountant's training progress. How can you not love Stanless Steel?

Stanley Pleskun, aka Stanless Steel, may not become a famous movie star, but he is a very strong man. Born on 10 May 1958, he has spent almost his entire life in South Brunswick, New Jersey, and currently lives in the same house where he was raised in Monmouth Junction, a rural part of South Brunswick. His interest in strength predates his earliest childhood memories, as his father told him he was trying to lift his own crib before it was time to leave it. Fascinated with Biblical stories of the strength of Samson, Stan was very active physically—wire-walking at age 10, progressing to walking on his hands, hand balancing, and lifting weights. As a youngster, he had the advantage and privilege of observing Joseph "the Mighty Atom" Greenstein during the twilight of his performing career when he appeared alongside Lawrence "Slim the Hammer Man" Farman. Stan and Slim go back almost 40 years.

> HIS INTEREST IN STRENGTH PREDATES THE EARLIEST OF CHILDHOOD MEMORIES, AS HIS FATHER TOLD HIM HE WAS TRYING TO LIFT HIS OWN CRIB BEFORE IT WAS TIME TO LEAVE IT.

Although skinny in his youth, Stanley eventually grew to the height of 6' 1" and has weighed as much as 295 lb., currently tipping the scales at around 255 lb. Stanless Steel (Pleskun's performing name for close to 20 years) was never a professional strongman or world-class powerlifter, but with a deadlift of 700 lb., squat of 550 lb., and bench press just under 500 lb. (raw), he has traditional strength skills respected by all. But it is the nontraditional in which Stan excels.

Some years back, I saw a photo in *MILO* ["Iron Filings," *MILO*, March 2004, Vol. 11, No. 4 (p. 62)] of a beefy fellow with dual Native American-style braids wearing a "Stanless Steel" sweatshirt. In 2005, at the first AOBS dinner I attended, I struck up a conversation with a now shorter-haired Stanley, still wearing his trademark clothing. Over the years, we became friends. I knew he was as strong as an ox, I knew he was a good steel bender, I knew that Slim Farman had known him for years, and from the number of video cameras that started rolling whenever he was in the hotel lobby with a piece of metal in his hands, I knew he had something going for him. But it wasn't until 2009 that I discovered just how special Stanley Pleskun is.

Although Stan has a successful demolition services business with employees, and because of his work has been in and out of 3,000 buildings in New Jersey and around New York City, he is a modern-day Luddite. In the Internet age, in a world where promoting oneself is increasingly dependent on the worldwide web, Stanley Pleskun, who during the 1990s was one of the most exposed and televised performing strongmen in the world, had fallen under the radar. Until 2009.

Before 2009, one of the few mentions of Stanless Steel on the web was a 1996 *New York Times* piece written prior to Stan's preventing two airplanes attached to his arms from taking off in opposite directions. The co-owner of the Princeton Airport said, "We're not going to have any arms pulling off, I have great faith in him." In 1999 at the same airport, NBC was on hand to film the same man performing the same stunt. The cameraman for NBC, a then

Stanless Steel does his trademark penny bend circa 2003.
Photo courtesy of Stan Pleskun.

25-year-old Columbia University graduate by the name of Zach Levy, was impressed enough to get Pleskun's phone number. Levy, who had also worked for *60 Minutes* and *Oprah* behind the camera, visited Stan in South Brunswick and knew what he wanted. Ten years later, he had finished his vision—only it took nine years longer than his original estimate. The result is a 113-minute documentary in the style of *cinema vérité*, an art form that uses no narration, captions, or music. Zach Levy's own story of the making of the film is fascinating and has been covered fairly extensively in film circles. The movie won the Grand Jury Prize at the 2009 Slamdance Film Festival and has received mostly favorable to fantastic critical reviews.

Strongman is not targeted at strength fans. Nevertheless, the film quality of some of the feat and stunt sequences is outstanding. Early in the film, the director obviously wanted to establish just how strong Stan is. There is a scene in a parking lot with a few hundred onlookers, where Stanless Steel leg presses the rear end of a truck weighing between 10,000 and 12,000 lb. Prior to the lift, the footage depicts a focused Stan pacing around, taking up the entire big screen. The inner fire burning in his eyes is beyond anything I have seen—in either fantasy characters or real people—not in Robert De Niro's character in *Raging Bull*, not in Dick Butkus chasing a ball carrier. You are not detached from the emotion, you practically feel its raw power. And that is in the opening five minutes.

After that, there are other strength scenes throughout the movie, but they are designed to weave into the director's story of personal struggle, common to all people, and not a strongman's triumph of strength. Although it may be what one would call an "arthouse film," strength fans get their fix as a byproduct.

What I learned from both the film and from talking to Stan himself is that Stanless Steel was a well-traveled performing strongman. The movie shows a very impressive one-finger deadlift of three people in something resembling an open elevator as Stanley hoists them upward from scaffolding. It took place on a popular television show in England and was a replica of a similar feat that Stan had done on a Japanese television show. When I asked what his favorite TV show on which he appeared was, Pleskun said, "That's easy. *Oddville, MTV*. I was on it three times. People were recognizing me wherever I went for years."

> YOU ARE NOT DETACHED FROM THE EMOTION, YOU PRACTICALLY FEEL ITS RAW POWER. AND THAT IS IN THE OPENING FIVE MINUTES.

Dennis Rogers, a well-known performing strongmen, stated on his website, "Stanley is also the best bender of partial movements in the world." In 2006, Slim Farman pulled out a partially bent piece of stainless steel that was 2" wide, 3/8" thick, and slightly over 1' long. As my son and I held it in our hands, Slim said that he did not think it could be bent, but Stanless Steel had done so. Not in the movie, but filmed by Levy, Pleskun's finest feat may have been bending into a "U" shape a 1/2" thick piece of rebar a bit over 9" long. It is now part of the strength museum at the University of Texas. Hopefully, someday, we will be able to see the footage of it being bent.

When asked which strength stars of the past he most admires, Stan is quick to rattle off his three favorites and why. First, the Mighty Atom. "I still don't know how he could bite through those nails." Second was Jack Walsh, an old-time strongman whom Stan met in a New Jersey gym. He taught Stanless the one-finger lift, lived with Stan for a while, and had unique and eclectic feats in his repertoire. Third was Vic Boff, founder of the Association of Oldetime Barbell and Strongmen (AOBS). Vic's ability to withstand the coldest day of the year's winter waters was to Stan an example of what one could do if he put his mind to it.

When Jack Walsh died in 2006 at the age of 77, the *New York Sun* ran a lengthy story that described quite a character. Besides performing traditional feats of strength, besides being, in the words of Zach Levy, "definitely a huge influence for Stan for the kinds of feats Stan does" (e.g., one-finger lifts and trucks driving on top of him), Walsh also billed himself as "The World's Strongest Man" for decades. The article mentioned feats completed, aborted, and evaded that included elephants, Mexican fighting bulls, and tugs of war with tugboats.

When I asked Stan, a close friend of Walsh, if it was true that there was a dent on top of Jack's head from standing with a barbell weighing over 500 lb. resting on top of it, Stan replied, "A dent? No, it was more like a groove, and a deep one, too." My personal take was that Jack Walsh was crazy. Others in the know have told me that Walsh was simply a performer who craved the money, women, and partying that sometimes went with it.

Stanless Steel is not a classic "performer" in the true sense of the word. Stan is not an illusionist and is an anti-showman, in that he does not make anything look easy. He candidly admits that he will take a feat to the point of failure. What he is most proud of is his work with coin bending, possibly only one of two or three people who can legitimately bend pennies with his fingers. As remarkable as that is, it is not a visibly impressive feat. Although happy with what he can do, Stan understands that some of what he does is not going to fill halls with spectators. To some degree, the movie speaks to that frustration. But the hardcore Iron Gamer has to appreciate that Stan has experienced what no other man has: he bent three pennies in front of the great John Grimek and Mr. Grimek was, to say the least, impressed.

> SLIM FARMAN, THE LAST OF THE TRUE OLD-TIME PERFORMING STRONGMEN, FLAT OUT TOLD ME STAN PLESKUN IS "SCARY." HE SAID THAT STAN "DOES NOT KNOW HE *CAN'T*."

Slim Farman, the last of the true old-time performing strongmen, flat out told me Stan Pleskun is "scary." He said that Stan "does not know he *can't*." That gives him an advantage over a normal person, in that he will take on a lift, bend, or feat with, in Slim's words, "the full intent of succeeding." Others know they cannot succeed and do not bother to attempt it. Not Stan.

About seven years ago, Stan's father died, and Stan decided it would be a good idea for his mind and spirit to go back to work. There was a 200-ton steam shovel that had not been moved in 75 years, and no contractor wanted to accept the job to dismantle it. The day after his father died, Stanley set out to work on it. He was cutting a 400-lb. piece off one of the arms of the equipment, and misjudged how it was attached. A large piece weighing more than 10,000 lb. swung down and struck Stan's back, knocking him to the ground and driving him into the dirt. As he was face down, bleeding from his back, his co-worker looked at him and passed out. Stan got up, picked up his friend, and rested a bit, and they went back to work. Doctors? Hospitals? Naah. Crazy? Naah. Steel-willed? You betcha. I asked why he took on that steam shovel job. "To prove I could do it," was his answer.

Over one hundred television appearances. Over a thousand live performances. Bending pennies at will. A vegetarian since age 12. The most impressive nail drive with the hand through a board and license plate you have ever seen (if you want an idea of what a gorilla's raw power would look

Stanless Steel was profiled in the September 1998 issue of *MILO*, when he was certified on the No. 3 Captains of Crush Gripper. This was the same issue that featured Bruce Webster, Jeff Maddy, and Jesse Marunde for certifying on the No. 3 Captains of Crush Gripper—how's that for putting Stan's accomplishment in context? Photo courtesy of Stan Pleskun/IronMind Enterprises, Inc.

like doing it, check out the movie trailer at www.strongmanfilm.com/trailer.html). Nail bending, spike bending, horseshoe bending. Featured in *People* magazine. Banana-bent a 5/8" thick elevator bolt under 14" long. Accomplished one-finger lifter. Chain breaker. Lifts weights outside, in New Jersey, during the cold winters. Bare-handed soda can bursting. Had the same truck drive on top of him more than ten times before a Los Angeles movie showing until the television crew got a good take. Allowed someone to film him more than 275 hours over a ten-year period. Madly in love with Barbara Hubbard for 12 years. Relationship meltdown on camera in a movie. Reconciliation of relationship off camera. The two watched some of the most unflattering scenes imaginable on the big screen, yet survived and grew. Certified on the No. 3 Captain of Crush Gripper (he was number 15) in 1998. One of the most genuinely unpretentious and nicest guys you'll ever meet.

Regardless of how history treats Stanley Pleskun as a performing strongman, there will never be an in-depth look at any Iron Gamer's life the way Zach Levy did it in *Strongman* with Stan. Because filming stopped in 2008, no one knows that in our worst economic times since the Great Depression, Pleskun has more work that he has ever had (and in the rough-and-tumble construction business of New Jersey and New York City notwithstanding). There are a lot of financial geniuses who can learn a thing or two from him.

I keep thinking about what Slim said about Stanley not knowing that he *can't*. For anyone to literally defy the laws of physics on a regular basis, it makes you wonder what are the possibilities for the rest of us with our lives, our communities, and beyond. Crazy? No, Stanless Steel is an accidental visionary.

M

IRON FILINGS

Randall J. Strossen, Ph.D. | *Publisher & Editor-in-chief*

Launching his boxing career with a bang, Arild "Emperor of Stones" Haugen knocked out Pavels Dolgos in 30 seconds of the first round, as the former top strongman brought his athletic talents and his ambition to the boxing arena in Spain.

To help focus for his fight, Arild Haugen told IronMind, "I didn't pay any attention to anything other than boxing and relaxing during the last days before the fight." And even though Haugen says, "It was fun," he was quick to add, "This is probably one of the hardest sports on Earth. It's a long way to go, but I am still young and hungry, so why not!? Limits are only in your head."

Asked why he had chosen boxing, rather than MMA, Haugen said, "I find boxing more exciting for me. Maybe I would have advanced faster in MMA because of my strength, but this just makes it more fun with boxing and more challenging for me. I think boxing is the purest and greatest area of fighting sports."

And as for his roots in strength sports, Arild Haugen told *MILO*, "I will never forget what strongman and the people in strongman did for me, either. They made me and without the strongman career, this wouldn't be so easy."

Arild isn't the only strongman star who has moved to a different strength realm. Five-time World's Strongest Man winner Mariusz

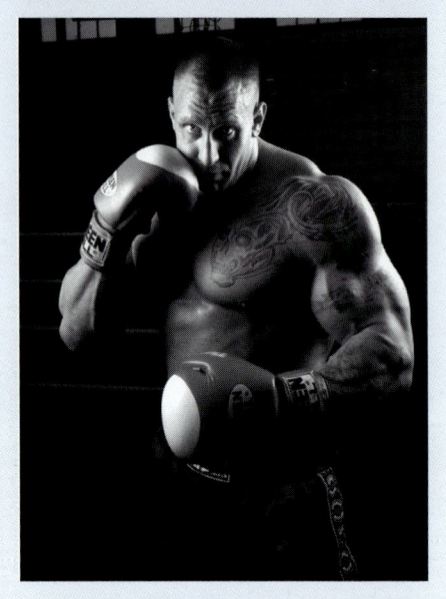

"I have been fascinated by boxing since I was a child," Arild Haugen told MILO.
Photo courtesy of Arild Haugen.

Pudzianowski is taking on the world of MMA. This is not as surprising as it might seem as, according to writer Phil Nourse of *Fighting Fit* magazine, Mariusz is a fourth-degree green belt in *Kyokushin karate* and has trained in combat sports for 11 years. If you want to read more about these strongman giants' forays into the world of combat, take a look at the December 2009/January 2010 issue of *Fighting Fit*, where Nourse has covered the moves in detail. M

In a not totally unexpected move, Olympic star Matthias Steiner was pulled from the 2009 World

Weightlifting Championships a week before the competition, and Frank Mantek, German National Weightlifting Coach, provided the explanation a in a formal statement.

Mantek gave three reasons for keeping the superstar home from Korea.

First, Matthias did not have sufficient recovery time from a groin operation in February 2009 to train adequately and regain world championship form.

Second, "after the Olympic Games in 2008 Matthias Steiner became a media darling in Germany." Winning and receiving honors—like Sportsman of the Year, the Saxon Salary Order (a very prestigious award in Saxony) World Weightlifter of the Year, and Bambi (the biggest German media prize)—and making countless TV appearances as a huge star took its toll on Matthias and his training.

Frank Mantek, himself an Olympic medalist in weightlifting, is the German National Weightlifting Coach.
Randall J. Strossen photo.

Mantek was optimistic that the attention would work in Matthias's favor in the future: "I am persuaded of the fact that [his winning] experiences will help him in it for the next year again to find the right priorities for the return to the world class in our sport."

Finally, Matthias's personal life has also changed, with a move to Heidelberg, a new girlfriend—and a biography that has created a great demand for his presence in many places.

"It has happened a lot," Mantek continued. "A young person has travelled the last year as quite a normal sportsman to Peking [Beijing] to come true a dream. From 19.08.2008 thus about 20.30 o'clock his life has totally changed." **M**

Jean-Louis Coppet, who also is the main organizer of the Bressuire Highland Games in France and the president of the French Highland Games Federation in association with the IHGF, reported that the heavy events training camp to bring more French blood to the sport was a major success. "There is a general agreement that traditional Highland Games in France are gaining ground," reported Francis Brebner.

Jean-Louis Coppet said, "We brought from Holland the charismatic Wout Zijlstra as coach to share his knowledge of the sport and its many techniques to the seven new French athletes who were kept very busy by Zijlstra the whole day, dedicating themselves to learning the process of heavy events. We've got a bunch of strong men, the enthusiasm is there,

Wout Zijlstra (back row, second from right) led a Highland Games training session in France, organized by Jean-Louis Coppet (back row, far right).
Photo courtesy of Francis Brebner.

[and we have] the right feeling and the proper love for Highland Games in Bressuire."

"Next year will see these budding athletes from [the] Bressuire [area] battle it out with other French throwers from Luzarches, France, in the IHGF French Highland Games championships to be held on 12–13 June 2010, which will run alongside the first ever IHGF World Heavy Events Super Series, which Bressuire is proudly hosting," Brebner told MILO.

Who's New

We've added two formidable gripsters to our No. 3 Captains of Crush Grippers certified list:

Jaime McEwen
Carlos F. Rivera

For a complete list of those certified on the No. 3, No. 3.5, and No. 4 Captains of Crush Grippers, or for the Rules for Closing and Certification, please visit the IronMind website at
www.ironmind.com.

Jaime McEwen established his position among the grip strength elite.
Photo courtesy of Jaime McEwen.

Jaime McEwen, 38 years old, 5' 11" and 225 lb., from Lancaster, New York, was "hooked" on grip training after being introduced to the No. 1 CoC Gripper by his father. After getting "stonewalled when I got the No. 3 about 3 years ago," Jaime began training with heavy kettlebell snatches and cleans, and thick-handled barbell and dumbbell lifts, and "noticed that the No. 3 suddenly became more obtainable. I've found that with the grippers, perseverance and experimentation have yielded favorable results . . . a more intuitive approach works for me. I can pretty much just feel when I'm going to have a good grip day." Married, with two daughters, Jaime is "going to start work on the No. 3.5 soon. From there we'll see what happens." We're betting on you, Jaime!

IronMind would like to thank Steven Helmicki for serving as the referee on Jaime McEwen's official attempt.

Carlos F. Rivera, the first Puerto Rican to be certified on the No. 3 CoC Gripper, hails from Vega Baja. At 27 years old, the 5' 11" 220-lb. business executive closed the No. 2 the first time he tried it. "I train 2–3 days a week . . . I like to mix different angles of gripping exercise" with

Carlos F. Rivera (r.) is now certified on the No. 3 Captains of Crush Gripper. Carlos Fernandez (l.), longtime IronMind customer, was Carlos's referee and wrote: "Mr. Rivera, after . . . closing a No. 3 gripper, proceeded to do the same with his left hand (a few times). It was very impressive and the audience loved it."
Photo courtesy of Carlos F. Rivera.

different pieces of grip equipment. Carlos has been an "active baseball player since I was six," and for that he trains for strength with weights, and for flexibility, endurance, coordination, reaction time, and eye–hand coordination exercises.

Since he discovered Captains of Crush Grippers "and other related gripping products such as the Rolling Thunder, I went from having 160 lb. of gripping pressure to 195 lb. I can see my improvement in my grip by watching balls flying much farther than I usually hit them." Carlos's goal is to certify on the No. 3.5. Congratulations on your achievement, Carlos, and welcome to the club!

IronMind would like to say a special thanks to Carlos Fernandez and the Golden Gym for their help with this certification—we appreciate it. **M**

Roster

Two short-steel benders have proven their mettle (and bent some metal) by certifying on IronMind's famed Red Nail:

Darin Heltemes
Dan Cenidoza

For a complete list of the Red Nail Roster and for the Rules and Certification for Bending a Red Nail, please visit the IronMind website at
www.ironmind.com.

It's official: Darin Heltemes has been certified on the IronMind Red Nail and his name added to the Red Nail Roster.
Photo courtesy of Darin Heltemes.

Darin Heltemes, of Fargo, North Dakota, told IronMind, "I started lifting weights 4 years ago as a scrawny 160-lb. weakling." Now this 30-year-old is a weakling no more—at 6' 0" and 230 lb., he credits his progress to the encouragement of his amateur strongman (and one ASC pro) friends. Darin "experimented with bending in my first year of lifting but abandoned it only after a month due to the extreme strain it places on the joints and tendons. I picked it back up three years later after my friend James gave me some steel for my birthday. . . . I bent my first Red Nail with the IronMind wraps four months after I began bending," Darin says. One of his main goals is to be able to bend the Red Nail in three ways: double overhand, double underhand, and reverse style. We're sure you'll reach your goals, Darin!

IronMind would also like thank Mark Wilson for his help in serving as Darin's official referee for this bend.

is proud to say that "the legendary John Brookfield has given me his blessing to carry on www.ironbonsai.com." Of his Red Nail bending feat, Dan's referee Marty Gallagher said, "Dan bent one nail in 15 seconds, then bent three in 60 seconds!" An impressive feat, indeed. Congratulations, Dan—your name has been added to the Red Nail Roster!

Special thanks to Marty Gallagher (ably backed by Rob Frye, his wife Alise, Sandy Sommer, Chris Hardy, Darius Gilbert, Mike Davis and Chuck Miller) for serving as the referee on Dan's official bend.

Marty Gallagher and the gang provided the context for Dan Cenidoza (third from left) officially bending the IronMind Red Nail.
Photo courtesy of Dan Cenidoza.

Dan Cenidoza is a 31-year-old strongman and trainer from Baltimore, Maryland. Owner of Be-More Training, Dan enjoys "bending metal, lifting heavy things, and long walks on the beach." At 6' 1" and 230 lb., this former winner of the Maryland's Strongest Man contest now focuses on strongman performances and feats of strength. Dan

Strength Contests at the Grass-Roots Level

New Page for Grip Strength in Russia: Rolling Thunder in Chelyabinsk

Sergey Klimakov

Russia's Uralstrong Federation, in cooperation with the Ural Center for Media Initiative, is beginning a series of amateur grip strength competitions, starting with a Rolling Thunder contest in Chelyabinsk. This initial competition was an amateur tournament for journalists, and more than twenty—from local newspapers, radio and television stations—met in an informal and friendly atmosphere at the Owl restaurant to test their own hand strength.

> This time the Armor, despite all her efforts, made only 50 kg on her pull. Marina was upset, but promised that she will work on strengthening her grip.

Strongwoman Marina "the Armor" Kigileva pulls a train engine . . . and tackles the Rolling Thunder. Anatoly Shulepov (train pull) and Sergey Klimakov (Rolling Thunder) photos, used with permission.

President of the Uralstrong Federation Dmitry Kononets was the judge and ensured that all the rules were met. All the participants had a go at the Rolling Thunder and the best results were a 55-kg pull for the men and a 32.5-kg pull for the women. The competition was fun and exciting for all who attended.

The highlight of the event was a personal record for strongwoman Marina "the Armor" Kigileva.

Dmitry Kononets said, "We know the current world record of [Britain's] Elizabeth Horne—65.5 kg. In training Marina took 55 kg, and she hoped to raise 60 kg, and even break the record of [the] Englishwoman." This time the Armor, despite all her efforts, made only 50 kg on her pull. Marina was upset, but promised that she will work on strengthening her grip.

"Marina 'the Armor' Kigileva is the women's face of the Uralstrong Federation and represents the first wave of Russian strongwomen. Thanks to the IronMind News column, we are able to closely watch the successes of strongwomen in the United States and Europe and we can see the results. We see the rapid development of a strongwoman sport in the world and we do not want to lag behind."

This year, Marina has set two outstanding records: the pull of an agricultural harvester (12.5 tons for 1.5 m) and the pull of a locomotive (175 tons for 10 m). In addition, in August she won the strongwoman tournament "Ural Battle," where she competed against the titled women's champion of weightlifting and powerlifting. M

Inaugural North American Highlander Association (NAHA) National Championships: Hybrid Format Going Strong

Thom Van Vleck

The first ever NAHA Nationals was held at Big Al Myers' legendary Dino Gym near Abilene, Kansas on 19 September 2009.

The Highlander format combines an equal number of strongman events and Scottish Highland Games events. The events selected for this year's National Championships included, from the strongman side, the farmer's walk, stone lifting, and a press medley. From the Highland Games side, the weight-over-bar, heavy hammer, and open stone were contested.

In perfect weather, nearly two dozen athletes from across the country took to the field. D. J. Satterfield and his partner, Richard "Vince" Vincent, had lined up a lot of great sponsors, giving the meet the big-time feel of a national-level contest. There were even cash prizes for the top three in each event.

The lightweight division was quite a battle and nothing was decided until going into the last event, the Atlas Stones. Justin Cantwell ended up with a one-point victory, barely hanging on over Matt Tyler. Mac Capello also edged out Matt Keller by one point for third place.

In the middleweight division, Mark Wechter took an early lead and never looked back with wins in 5 of 6 events, showing domination in strongman and Highland Games heavy events.

In the heavyweight division, Matt Vincent had a dominating performance along with some huge throws. Matt really showed great all-around athletic ability that will make him a tough Highlander champion to dethrone. His 53' 4-1/2" open stone put was amazing!

NAHA National Championships competitors.
Al Myers photo

The masters' division saw John O'Brien take an early lead and hold off Clint Garda and Thom Van Vleck who were second and third. Even though John found out he couldn't lose mathematically going into the last event, he was still the only master to load all five stones, putting a punctuation mark on his victory.

The Highlander format, once again, showed the athletes must be proficient in both strongman and Highland Games, not just one sport. As NAHA continues to grow, with 15 state chairs and 11 state- and national-level meets in its first year, it will be interesting to see what 2010 will bring. ∎

Learning from the Best: Ryan Vierra Throws Clinic Gives a Big Return on the Investment

Ryan Seckman

Arizona Scottish Games
Athletic Director

On January 2, 2010, John Teets Park in Phoenix, Arizona was home to the final installment of the Ryan Vierra throws clinics put on with John Godina, the four-time world champion and three-time Olympian in the shot put. Ryan Vierra, five-time Highland Games world champion, again delivered more than was promised to those in attendance by bringing along his longtime friend and Highland Games legend Francis Brebner. Francis put his own spin on each event and his participation allowed for an even greater dialogue between coaches and athletes to find different physical and mental cues to advance the throwing ability of each individual.

The clinic started with the weights-for-distance. With notebooks, cameras and video recorders in hand, the 15 athletes who made the investments in their futures listened intently to what Ryan and Francis had to say. Ryan Vierra and Francis Brebner are world-class in the weights-for-distance. Francis, who retired from competition a few years ago, still holds the second-best ever recorded 28-lb. weight toss over 94'. Each athlete went through the stages of the throw: from the first movement, the setup for the sprint toward the throwing area, through to the extension needed in the legs to maximize the catapult effect you want at the finish.

Hammers were the next topic, and we worked on things like establishing a low point based on 0 and 180 degrees, while Francis keyed in on the need to work the hammer across the body from 8 o'clock to 4 o'clock, respectively, to maximize the distance. Thankfully, lunch and rest came as the third event, and we gladly made the most of that time with needed energy replacement from the intense drills and throwing we did from 8:30 to noon.

Part two of our day started with John Godina, who worked with us on staying on our right or left, depending on our throwing hand, initiating the movement with our driving leg, extending and turning the heel, and ending with both legs fully extended.

The reason a thrower would want to fully extend the legs was shown to us, with John having us do a standing jump for height. He asked us to do the jump without extending up on our toes first and then with the extension. It was easy to see that you cannot get the full effect of the movement without fully extending on the toes.

John has recently established the World Throws Center in Phoenix, offering world-class facilities and coaching for those wishing to have the very best training available in the world.

The caber was up next and the group got a taste of the Arizona specialty cabers, which are costly and time-intensive to make. Due to our lack of humidity and very hard ground, we have resorted to covering the natural wood cabers with fiberglass so that the cabers will last longer than one practice. These cabers have turned out to save time and effort with the four Arizona Games that are held throughout the year.

Arizona pro Andrew Hobson and three-time women's world champion Summer Pierson are great examples of what it means to be a true pro. They were a joy to watch during this part of the clinic, showing that even the best have something to learn. With coaching from Ryan and Francis, they both improved on the caber, as did the entire group. Every piece of advice from the coaches only increased their will to get the cabers to turn.

Athletes and coaches at the Ryan Vierra throws clinic, from left: Francis Brebner, Ryan Vierra, Kirstie Abbott, Glen Adams, David Voth, Richard Kahle, Andrew Hobson, Summer Pierson, Ryan Seckman, Jacob Darling, Mike Melia, Ryan Puckett, and West Imboden.
Photos courtesy of Ryan Seckman.

The day was winding down—or so we thought—as we had been at the park learning and throwing from early in the morning until 4 p.m.—when we turned to the weight-over-bar. Soon we found out that weight-over-bar is not an event for the fainthearted. At one point during an attempt, Ryan reminded us that this is a violent movement and even said you had to think of it as a life-or-death moment during your attempt. Of course, mostly this was to get the athletes to concentrate so that they could have a single focus, tuning out what else was going on. While his advice was said in jest, it showed the seriousness of a moment in competition for those like Ryan and Francis.

That second wind from the weight-over-bar was exactly what we needed to finish the day with the first-ever Scottish Games Rolling Thunder competition in Arizona. Francis Brebner was the official judge, and IronMind was kind enough to send the Rolling Thunder contest equipment to us so that it would be official.

We started with 90 lb. so that those who had not attempted this lift would get to try it before it got too serious. I could not believe how heavy it felt, as the handle rotated no matter what I tried to do to get a grip. Most of the group succeeded in the 90-lb. deadlift so we felt we should go up by 35 lb.—that was when the competition narrowed down to a smaller group and became more serious. After each round we added 10 lb. until we got to two final athletes—Richard Kahle, a powerlifter from southern New Mexico, and Andrew Hobson, the local pro Highland Games athlete. The athletes matched each other in weight and intensity at each level until the weight of 175 lb. was loaded onto to the equipment. Andrew Hobson was first up and succeeded on his first attempt. Richard came so close on all three attempts that the words "good lift" were coming out of the judge's mouth just as the weight would crash down. Congratulations to Andrew! **M**

Highland Games heavy Andrew Hobson was the winner of the Rolling Thunder contest.

King Beowulf and The Dragon's Lair:
Are You Ready?

William Crawford, M.D.

The aging King Beowulf had enjoyed years of peace as the king of Geatland. No longer the lusty young warrior who craved glory and adventure, Beowulf faced another challenge later in life with all the dangers that were entwined in his epic battle with the Grendel. At the end of the epic of Beowulf, a sleeping dragon was awakened and was attacking the aging monarch's kingdom, even his very home. All honor and glory of the past were on the line as his legacy depended on his ability to face this foe and protect his people.

Just as with Beowulf, nature's invariable disinterest in the plight of men causes even the strongest among us to age. We have the Grendel's arm on our mantel, but how many of us have to now face the dragon? Do we go gently into our aging years or do we stand and fight? MILO readers are special and no doubt many of you know where this is going. Will you continue to struggle against the foe, which is the ticking clock of time, or will you let the dragon take you? Will you fight? Why do I ask?

> DO WE GO GENTLY INTO OUR AGING YEARS OR DO WE STAND AND FIGHT?

We all train to keep our strength, but do we push our cardiovascular system to its limit to keep the beating heart of a warrior? Do we keep our heart strong to match the strength of our grip, the same grip that allowed us to defeat the Grendels of our youth? It is easy to not push ourselves to drive up our heart rates to a limit that approaches the dragon's lair, a place that men of average courage dare not explore.

I intend to go into the dragon's lair and claim victory but, unlike our hero Beowulf, I do not intend to make this a battle of mortal combat. Instead, as with many of you, I want to maintain my ability to train to stay strong. But again, the key is to condition our cardiovascular systems to match our strength—and then forge ahead with the conditioning to be stronger still.

Hopefully the above words will inspire all of you to challenge yourselves in your later years. The point of this article is to give some guidelines for a safe way to pursue this conditioning. Specifically, what is a safe maximal heart rate to use as a guideline for cardiovascular conditioning? Do you need to push yourself to a maximal heart rate to gain the benefits of conditioning? What are your expectations and goals? Do you have medical or physical limitations? Are you limited by fear, apprehension, or good old-fashioned laziness? Read on.

As a rule of thumb, the target heart rate to achieve a cardiovascular training effect (training to increase cardiac output) lies in a simple equation. I have given this formula in a previous issue of *MILO* ["Blood Pressure: By the Numbers," June 2003, Vol. 11, No. 1], but here it is again. Subtract your age from 220 and you'll get your maximum heart rate. A quick example: if you are 50 years old, 220 − 50 = 170 beats per minute (bpm). The target rate is 70–80% of your maximum heart rate; thus, for this example, it is 119–136 bpm. This target heart rate needs to be achieved and maintained for 20 minutes 3 times per week. Again, this is for a training effect and frankly, for most of us, we need to work up to this level of conditioning. If you cannot achieve this goal, are you wasting your time? Of course not.

Walking 30 to 60 minutes 3 to 5 times per week has proven to reduce bodyweight, decrease resting pulse, and even decrease blood pressure. A renowned article in *The Journal of the American Medical Association* revealed that running reduced the relative risk of a cardiovascular event by over 40%. Walking decreased the relative risk by 25%, and weight training 3 times per week also reduced the relative risk by 25%.

Studies are underway to determine the relative reduction in risk factor when combining weight training and walking; intuitively, it is thought that it will lower the relative risk even more than each one of the exercise types would alone. Stay tuned for the results.

What about a "safe" target heart rate? Is it possible that a heart rate can be too elevated to be called safe? In a word, yes—but only in special circumstances. I will digress to remind those of you who have not been undergoing any conditioning work to check with your physician first, particularly if you have a prior medical condition. A stress test can give valuable information regarding the safety of a cardiovascular conditioning program. A heart rate that is too high to be safe can be considered a *tachyarrthymia*. To simplify, a tachyarrthymia is a sustained irregular heart rate after stopping exercise, usually over 120 bpm for over 3 minutes, which is dangerous. But again, a tachyarrthymia is a medical condition and is not usually achieved by merely pushing yourself. If you cannot find your breath after exercise, this could be a tachyarrthymia.

Another condition that can occur and is responsible for up to 50% of sudden cardiac deaths in athletes is *hypertrophic cardiomyopathy*. This is a genetic condition where the heart muscle thickens, which restricts blood flow through the heart and can even cause the heart to stop suddenly. If you have had chest pain, lightheadedness, or palpitations, or have passed out while exercising, you should seek medical attention. If you have a family member who has died suddenly while exercising or if you have a personal history or family history of heart murmurs, again you need to be evaluated by a physician. An echocardiogram is an ultrasound of the heart, a non-invasive test that can diagnose hypertrophic cardiomyopathy. There are treatments for this condition, but they are usually directed by a cardiologist.

As for the exercise stress test, the physician performing the examination will push you to achieve a target heart rate for your age to ascertain if an adequate test has been performed. Specifically, the doctor will push you to elevate your heart rate (usually while walking on a treadmill) to see how your heart reacts to exercise as measured by your heart rate, blood pressure, and EKG tracings. Those parameters, combined with symptoms of chest pain, disproportionate breathlessness or lightheadedness, can detect heart disease in an otherwise asymptomatic person—good information from just a few minutes on a treadmill.

I have written in MILO previously about coronary artery disease and heart attacks, hypertension and high cholesterol. Conditioning is a way to stave off these problems. Along with the fact that being overweight, developing high blood pressure, and even developing diabetes can be thwarted by starting some conditioning, you will feel better, too.

By the way, I have also contributed to MILO in the past about metabolic syndrome, aka syndrome X ["Metabolic Syndrome: Does This Sound Familiar?" December 2006, Vol. 14, No. 3]. Metabolic syndrome is defined as obesity, glucose intolerance, hypertension, and high cholesterol levels. Each factor on its own may not be too dangerous, but all these conditions together are deadly. Again, the prescription for metabolic syndrome is exercise and some moderation in eating habits. In one medical study, a decrease in weight of 5 to 10% allowed more than half of those participating in the study to stop or reduce medications for high blood pressure or diabetes.

Generally then, you can push yourself to reach these new cardiovascular conditioning levels. Again, after consulting with your physician and having no symptoms such as chest pain or lightheadedness, the green light is on!

What is your expectation? To feel better? To increase your conditioning level to achieve fitness for a sport? To lose some weight? The question then becomes, how do you tailor your program to fit your needs? I have some basic recommendations.

First, find a sustainable type of exercise program—exercises that will build you up and not set you up for failure. Pick exercises that hold your interest.

Second, approach the goal of improved conditioning as you do your other strength goals. If you want to deadlift 600 lb., you build up to that level of strength—you don't put 600 lb. on the bar and keep tugging on it and hope one day it comes off the floor. Start slowly and work up to a new conditioning level.

Third, be realistic. Some of us cannot squat due to some type of injury, but we find ways around that obstacle. Jogging is a great exercise, but maybe not something you think you would benefit from. Walking is a great alternative, as are many other activities. However, don't sell yourself short— maybe you *can* jog and not just tell yourself, "I can't."

Squat thrust press exercise: Start in a standing position with the dumbbells; drop down to the floor to a squat thrust with the dumbbells in hand; jump up from the down position; and clean the dumbbells, ready to either press the dumbbells overhead or restart the sequence. Repeating the sequence quickly for 10 to 20 reps gives the desired training effect. Photos courtesy of Bill Crawford.

Fourth, incorporate conditioning into your program of strength training. If you think conditioning is all or nothing, you will resent the conditioning workouts if you completely stop strength training. Make conditioning part of your strength training. As an example, I have recently undertaken a 4-week 20-rep squat routine. My heart rate increased to over 140 bpm after the 20-rep set (and this was after I was lucid enough to take my pulse). Anyone who has done the 20-rep squat routine can attest to the steam-engine breathing and heart-pounding that this routine can generate—it is a great combination of strength and endurance training.

The above 20-rep squat routine then led to incorporating some jogging into my workout and so far this is working well. It's modest jogging, truth be told, about a mile at a fairly slow pace 3 times per week, and to ramp up my heart rate and add a strengthening component to the jogging, I do some sprints in the workout. Just to let you know, I have been going for these little jaunts just after stone lifting. I am sure my neighbors are gathering the children to safety after seeing a pretty large human covered in chalk and dirt jogging down the street.

A point of interest to me is that anthropological research suggests that running was used by our distant ancestors to acquire meat. These primordial humans didn't have to run down a plant, but they did have to run to hunt. Think about it: spend a little time on the plains of Africa and watch who runs—the animals who want meat and the animals who do not want to be meat. The carnivore in you, the caveman in you says it's okay to move your lower limbs faster than a walking pace with no shame involved.

A personal favorite of mine is carrying stones (hey, wow, Bill, no kidding!). Carrying stones, like the Husafell stone, is a strength-endurance feat. What is the limiting factor for many a strong man who attempts to carry a heavy stone? You got it, they run out of gas. If you don't have the hand and back strength to lift the stone, then the cardiovascular component is not a factor. But if you have the strength to lift the stone and start on the way, your heart-lung machine is quickly taxed. Lightheadedness, heavy breathing, and even blacking out can occur without the endurance to push ahead when attempting to carry a heavy slab.

Another idea for conditioning is John Brookfield's Battling Ropes system, personally shown to me by John and previously described in MILO ["Battling Ropes Basics" by John Brookfield, September 2008, Vol. 16, No. 2]. The ropes routines are devastatingly effective and are a sustainable exercise in that they are a low-impact pursuit. Battling Ropes movements also increase explosiveness and develop strength, particularly grip strength. John describes elevating his heart rate to over 200 bpm. After having had the pleasure of doing some training with him, I know he is the real thing as he exhausted me in a short amount of time and he kept on moving.

A great exercise that my friend Erik Sauve showed me is something he calls STP, short for squat thrusts and presses. Take a pair of dumbbells, fairly light to start, and place them on the floor. Reach down and take the dumbbells from the floor to the chest and press them overhead. Put the dumbbells back on the floor, drop down into a push-up position, jump back between the dumbbells and stand (the squat thrust portion of the exercise). Perform 10 repetitions. This is a great way to round out a strength training session as your heart will be pounding after this exercise. Tire flipping, sled dragging, pounding a sledgehammer onto a tire, sprinting, kettlebell training, weight vest training, and on and on—with the number of possible exercises that are fun and highly effective, there is no excuse for not incorporating conditioning into our routines.

Beowulf went to the dragon's lair and was victorious over a creature of epic proportions. This allegory is man overcoming his old age and fear to rise again to struggle. Surely the aging warrior in us can do the same and reach new heights in conditioning as well as strength. **M**

> THINK ABOUT IT: SPEND A LITTLE TIME ON THE PLAINS OF AFRICA AND WATCH WHO RUNS—THE ANIMALS WHO WANT MEAT AND THE ANIMALS WHO DO NOT WANT TO BE MEAT.

Overtraining—Symptoms, Causes, Prevention

Ernest Roy, P.T., D.P.T.

If you train for the purpose of competition, even if the competition is against your own personal bests, you may be flirting with overtraining. Many athletes have done more than simply flirt with it—a few unfortunate souls have even moved in with it and set up house. On a mild level, overtraining can ruin a good training cycle. When it hits full force, it can lead to physical and emotional burnout, injury, and even emotional depression. Sports science classifies overtraining in various stages. Let's review what is known about this condition as it applies to strength sports, and learn how to identify the symptoms and causes and how to avoid or manage it if it happens to you.

General adaptation syndrome (GAS)

All training creates stress on the body. Generally, this stress is beneficial and stimulates a response from the body, causing improvements in physical performance, such as strength, muscle size, or power. Much of our knowledge of how the body responds to stress and stimulus comes from the pioneering research of physiologist Hans Selye. Dr. Selye proposed a theory that has come to be known as the general adaptation syndrome (GAS). A great deal of research on how the human body responds to various stresses has come down from Dr. Selye's original work.

The theory states that the body will maintain a steady state, called homeostasis, in the absence of any outside influence to change. Simply put, if you don't train, you don't get any stronger. When an athlete trains, the workout acts as a disruptive force to this steady state. All the research and experiments on strength throughout the ages have simply been an effort to better learn how to get the body to adapt more efficiently to training. Provided there are adequate rest and nutrition, the body will adapt to the stress of the workout by growing stronger. If enough of the requirements for adequate adaptation are not met, then strength gains will not happen. When an athlete continues to force the body to go through further stresses, the problem can worsen. The ultimate example of inadequate adaptation to stresses would be the death of the organism. Let's assume that most *MILO* readers are highly motivated trainers, but not crazy enough to train to the point of dropping dead.

> WHEN AN ATHLETE TRAINS, THE WORKOUT ACTS AS A DISRUPTIVE FORCE TO THIS STEADY STATE.

What is overtraining?

The mildest form of overtraining is known as overreaching, which actually is often used intentionally as a training technique. It works by purposely inserting a sudden significant increase in training load into a training cycle.

The idea is to provide a fresh stimulus to spur later gains in strength. As an example, let's say that my usual system is to squat once per week. I may use 4 to 5 sets with reps of 3 to 6. To insert an overreaching mini-cycle into my program, I work the squats twice in a given week, using a total of 12 work sets for the week, with reps of 3 to 5, thus doubling my volume (assuming I use weights similar to the prior week).

One must understand the increased training load is of short duration, usually in two to three workouts at most. By doing this, I may well find a burst of progress with my planned 1-rep max attempt 4 to 6 weeks down the line. This is sometimes referred to as a residual or delayed transformation effect from a training program. Obviously, the athlete would try to time the overreaching cycle in an effort to experience the performance burst as close to an important competition as possible.

Overtraining *per se* has been defined as any increase in load, intensity, or volume that causes a long-term reduction in performance. By long-term, we are talking about weeks or potentially even several months. Typically, it is not strictly a training program problem. Other factors often are influential in the development of the overtraining syndrome. Outside emotional stress, illness, lack of sufficient restorative methods, or other energy drains all can be strong contributors to the problem. Ironically, the research on the overtraining syndrome has typically focused more on aerobic or endurance-style sports, such as swimming, running, or long-distance cycling. Some of the typical physical signs and symptoms reported as indicators of overtraining in aerobic athletes, like increases in the resting pulse or blood pressure, may not be accurate or consistent enough for strength sports.

Research has gleaned a few useful clues as to the physiological mechanisms associated with overtraining. There appear to be different pathways where overtraining can occur. One is as a result of excessive volume that overwhelms the athlete's recuperative powers. This simply means too many workouts, repetitions, sets, or some combination of these factors. The problem can also develop as a result of using intensity levels that are too high to sustain for too long a period of time.

The problem may be compounded when excessive volume and intensity are rolled together, which happens when athletes adopt the mistaken belief that more is always better. If your bench press is moving along nicely by doing 3 working sets twice per week, will adding 6 sets each of flyes, dips, cable crossovers, and inclines give you a better result? Maybe. But then again, maybe not. Unless you are a genetic freak, on steroids, or both, 6- to 7-days-per-week workout routines, lasting 3 to 4 hours per day with nonstop high intensity (working to failure or close to it), will likely break you down in short order. Ronnie Coleman's triple split pre-Mr. Olympia workout makes for dramatic reading in the muscle magazines. If you try to prepare for the

> THE PROBLEM MAY BE COMPOUNDED WHEN EXCESSIVE VOLUME AND INTENSITY ARE ROLLED TOGETHER, WHICH HAPPENS WHEN ATHLETES ADOPT THE MISTAKEN BELIEF THAT MORE IS ALWAYS BETTER.

state powerlifting meet with this type of workout, you'll probably end up lifting more like your grandmother.

High-intensity training has been associated with certain changes in levels of endocrine hormone activity in the body. Prior research identified increases in levels of adrenaline and noradrenaline hormones with chronic high-intensity overtraining. On the contrary, high-volume overtraining was marked by decreases in testosterone levels along with decreases in the testosterone/cortisol ratio. These are all extremely important hormones involved in regulating how well our neuromuscular structures recuperate and perform under stress. Notice I said neuromuscular. Your central nervous system has a great deal of influence in how well you adapt to training. Much of the adaptation to strength training involves improved efficiency of the central nervous system at firing large numbers of muscles in an increasingly efficient manner. Unless you have access to regular blood testing, you will not likely be able to identify these types of hormone changes yourself. This type of testing requires a laboratory and could become rather expensive if repeated frequently.

Before going further, I would like to briefly touch on a relatively rare condition that you may not have heard of. It is known as rhabdomyolysis and is a potentially deadly form of sudden overtraining. It is essentially a massive breakdown of muscle protein, known as myoglobin. This typically occurs with a sudden, extreme spike in training intensity. Although it has often been associated with poor fluid intake or dehydration, that is not a necessary prerequisite. Signs to watch out for include unusual or extreme muscle pain and an unmistakable dark brown color to the urine. The colored urine indicates that significant muscle damage has occurred and degraded protein is being excreted. Should you experience these symptoms, get to an emergency room as soon as possible. The excessive amounts of degraded protein in the urine can actually result in clogging the renal tubules, leading to kidney failure and possible death. A recently published research paper documented a case of this occurring in an 18-year-old college football player. The athlete was put through a workout by a certified trainer at the college he was attending. Among other things, the workout consisted of at least 300 repetitions of squats using heavy rubber tubes as resistance. Fortunately, the young man took himself to a hospital in time and after approximately a week of inpatient care, he recovered fully.

Signs of overtraining

What are signs and symptoms that you should be aware of in order to avoid the basic overtraining problem? Here's a short checklist for you to consider:

Signs of overtraining

- prolonged lack of desire to train and the lack of overall drive: although this is subjective, most well-motivated athletes will immediately recognize this change in their focus and concentration level. Don't confuse this with laziness (I know there are no lazy *MILO* readers, right?)
- reduced appetite
- difficulty obtaining restful sleep, or even insomnia
- reduced resistance to infection–are you getting sick more than usual?
- stiffness or muscle soreness that seems unusual or excessive: you may find that your normal warm-up routine is insufficient to alleviate the soreness from your last workout. In some cases athletes reported symptoms similar to those seen with clinical depression, including lack of interest in

Signs of overtraining (cont.)

other people close to you, such as family or friends. The athlete may experience a sadness or general anxiety that appears for no apparent reason
- noticeable loss in strength: you may find that you are suddenly getting drilled by weights that you previously handled comfortably
- noticeable loss in stamina: you may experience onset of fatigue more rapidly than usual during workouts. Three sets of squats may result in exhaustion, where previously you had done 6 to 8 sets

Preventing overtraining

How does one prevent overtraining? You should alternate your routine in a planned manner. Constantly juggle your sets, repetitions, and intensity levels. Keep a training journal: this will allow you to track your progress and evaluate prior training routines. You should note things such as your energy levels on a weekly basis in your journal.

One thing that you have to realize is that high-level elite athletes do not train like maniacs all year long. Many elite Olympic lifters report an average training intensity around 80% of their 1-rep maximum. Save the really high-intensity stuff for just before your most important meets. I have found as I age (48 years at present), that I do better if I limit myself to no more than two consecutive weeks of training a major lift at 90% or more of my 1-rep max. Certainly when in my twenties, I could drill high-intensity loads more often. I still feel, however, that it was wrong to do so even then, and I firmly believe that I could have progressed better and avoided injury by cycling those loads in a more judicious manner.

After any competition or really grueling cycle, insert a low-intensity week (often called an unloading mini-cycle) to your program. Then, slowly ramp the loads back up in a wavelike fashion. Here's a simple chart of what this might look like for a squat cycle.

Week	1	2	3	4	5	6
Sets/reps	3 x 8–10	5 x 5	3 x 3	3 x 2	3 x 5	1–3 x 1
Load	60–70%	75–80%	80–85%	90+%	85%	100+%

There are no magic rep-set-load numbers. The variations you could use are almost infinite. You have to know yourself and monitor your program. I strongly believe in competitive athletes taking a one-week training hiatus every 4 months to allow themselves to refresh their physical and emotional batteries. Try it. You won't wither away to 120 lb. after one week out of the gym. What you will notice is a renewed ferocity and a likely burst of progress when you do resume training.

Watch outside energy drains. If your job has you pulling overtime hours, you may need to make some adjustments in the gym. If you experience a sudden surge in life stress (illness or death in the family, divorce, or job loss, just to name a few) take care to pay attention to the impact these can have on your available energy. You may need to explore better relaxation or recuperation measures. Some find techniques such as massage or meditation very helpful in managing stress. Instead of going out every other night until 1 a.m., maybe just kicking back with a cold one and watching a ball game in your living room would be helpful.

> . . . MAYBE JUST KICKING BACK WITH A COLD ONE AND WATCHING A BALL GAME IN YOUR LIVING ROOM WOULD BE HELPFUL.

Weightlifting and Blood Pressure

Dezso Ban

"Weightlifting-induced hypertension" is a fiction that started as a rumor which spread and became accepted as truth. Weightlifting was deemed a threat to cardiovascular health and was denounced by the omnipotent, self-appointed health authorities by agreement, not by investigation.

But that theory is not profound: it does not contribute to the understanding of how lifting affects blood pressure and it is not supported by evidence or logic. The accusers don't even make an attempt to describe the mechanism of their theory, and conveniently ignore the fact that the occurrence of hypertension among weightlifters is not higher than among the general population. Furthermore, their claim contradicts another one for the same heart function, namely the beneficial effects of running. Actually, the heart of the runner and the heart of the lifter have the same task, effective blood delivery. The runner's task is through pumping large volumes, the weightlifter's is through more forceful pumping. Both are adaptive responses, the results of improved heart efficiency; therefore, both are beneficial.

Recovering from overtraining

If you do experience a prolonged period of fatigue in the gym and notice a lack of energy and motivation, you may be experiencing a full-blown overtraining episode. The only treatment at that point is a period of rest. This does not necessarily mean stopping all physical activity. It is often better to engage in active rest—this would mean significantly reduced volume and intensity of your workouts. Training would become more of a playful thing, or you might simply opt to engage in less intense physical activities for a period of time.

How long might recovery take? This will depend on how deeply you have dug a hole for yourself. Severe overtraining may require several weeks to several months for full recovery. Short-term overreaching can be absorbed in a normal training program and will often result in improved performance several weeks later.

The best way to handle overtraining is to not fall into the trap in the first place. Plan your workouts logically. Monitor your energy levels and emotional state. Have an annual physical checkup. If you notice abnormal changes in your normal energy levels, tell your physician. In some cases, an underlying health problem may be the culprit. Conditions such as heart disease, diabetes, low testosterone level, hypothyroidism, depression, or severe emotional stress can be present with unexplained fatigue as a symptom. Arm yourself with knowledge, know your body, and don't be afraid to ask questions if things don't seem right. ∎

The human body is analogous to a closed, pressurized fluid circuit. It is composed of a cardiovascular system: heart as the pump, arteries and veins as the transport vessels, blood as the transport fluid, and body organs as the resistors. (A resistor is a circuit element that restrains fluid transport.) If any component malfunctions, its resistance will change and cause a corresponding change in the total resistance of the circuit, thereby a change in the fluid (blood) pressure. The nerve centers control the functions of all the components. Many things can go wrong, but the body is a wonderful machine—its design is just about perfect. If taken care of, it rarely breaks down and its maintenance is quite simple. All it needs are nourishment, exercise, and rest. When prudence and moderation are practiced in addition, health is preserved.

If the exercise chosen is weightlifting, the improvement in physiological efficiency will be substantial. Injuries can happen, however, adding resistance to the circulatory system. The resulting increase in blood pressure cannot be construed as hypertension for, upon recovery, the injury-caused resistance is removed and the blood flow returns to normal. Nevertheless, resistance increase in the blood circuit is the necessary condition for blood pressure increase. It is required by fluid dynamics.

Cardiovascular function obeys the law of physics. Accordingly, one or more of the following changes must be permanently present in the circulatory system in order for the resistance to increase and cause hypertension:

1. increase in blood volume
2. increase in blood viscosity
3. increase in blood density
4. increase in the size or decrease in the elasticity of the body organs
5. impairment of the circulatory system or of the body's tension–relaxation mechanism
6. decrease in the volume of the blood vessels
7. decrease in the volumes of the heart chambers

Clearly, weightlifting cannot cause 1, 2, 3, or 5. As for 4, increasing the size or decreasing the elasticity of the body organs, weightlifting can increase the muscle mass, thereby increasing the resistance of the circulatory system. But this is compensated for by the improved vascularity and elasticity of the skeletal and the cardiac muscles.

> MANY THINGS CAN GO WRONG, BUT THE BODY IS A WONDERFUL MACHINE—ITS DESIGN IS JUST ABOUT PERFECT.

Number 6 requires a degenerative change, such as arteriosclerosis, to impede blood flow. But weightlifting facilitates blood flow by maintaining the strength and suppleness of the blood vessels. The idea that it happens at the expense of cardiovascular efficiency is an oxymoron. If 7 could occur, it would cause an accelerated pulse rate, but no observation supports this. The claim that weightlifting causes a decrease in the heart chambers' volumes has never been proven, and it is the denial of the body's adaptability. However, bad ideas die hard, and it may take some time for reason to prevail. The truth will eventually be decided by facts, not by allegations.

Rigorous investigation shows "weightlifting-induced hypertension" is an effect without a cause; the "theory" thus violates the principles of physics and causality. Hypertension is a serious concern, but weightlifting is not a cause of it. Frivolous allegations must not deter people from participating in an activity which is in fact beneficial. Actually, weightlifting is the best activity a person can do to improve and preserve health.

The argument can be made that weightlifting lowers blood pressure. A comparison with running could be used to show this. During running, oxygen use is large but the resistances the heart has to overcome are not. The runner's heart works against moderately elevated resistance. Moderately increased blood pressure will therefore be sufficient to deliver even a large supply of blood. The heart will adapt: its chambers will enlarge, it will become somewhat stronger, and will be able to deliver more blood per minute. When the running stops, both the blood circuit resistance and the need for oxygen become normal. To avoid oversupplying blood, the pulse rate slows down, which causes the blood pressure to drop.

In contrast, during lifting, the oxygen consumption is only moderate but the blood circuit resistance is large. Much increased blood pressure is required to deliver even a moderately increased blood supply. The heart will adapt: it will become stronger, larger, more muscular, and will be able to develop pressures to overcome even large resistances in order to deliver blood. When lifting is over, the body's resistance decreases and the need for blood becomes normal. The pumping force and pulse rate drop to avoid oversupplying blood, thus causing the blood pressure to drop. Blood pressure is thus both resistance and pulse-rate dependent.

The heart has one function only—pumping blood. It is not meaningful to claim that this function works one way for the runner and another way for the lifter. The work that both their hearts perform is blood delivery under somewhat different conditions because of the different demands: much increased blood supply and moderately elevated blood pressure for the runner; and moderately increased blood supply and much elevated blood pressure for the lifter. When their activities are over and increases in blood supply and pressure are no longer needed, things return to normal. The runner's heart rate slows down, and the weightlifter's heart pumps with less force; as a result their blood pressures drop. By inference I conclude that weightlifting reduces blood pressure. M

> HYPERTENSION IS A SERIOUS CONCERN, BUT WEIGHTLIFTING IS NOT A CAUSE OF IT.

> WHEN THEIR ACTIVITIES ARE OVER AND INCREASES IN BLOOD SUPPLY AND PRESSURE ARE NO LONGER NEEDED, THINGS RETURN TO NORMAL.

German Men of Might:
Alois Selos

Gherardo Bonini

Alois Selos.
Courtesy of Gherardo Bonini.

In Germany, for some years after the great Hans Beck's retirement there were no improvements in the weightlifting records and in the challenge to Austrian lifters for the leadership position he vacated. The hopeful Heinrich Neuhaus was obliged to stop his career. Alois Selos was the man who took on Beck's heritage and challenged the new Austrian star Steinbach [see *MILO*, September 2004, Vol. 11, No. 2: "The Unrecognized Hero of Austrian Weightlifting: Josef Steinbach"].

Selos was born in 1875, and in 1898 he dedicated himself to weightlifting, joining the *Erste Männer Stemmklub München-Augsburg* (First Men Lifting Club for Munich–Augsburg). He was a butcher by trade, and even from the beginning he was famous for his size. Standing 1.72 m (5' 8") tall and weighing 125 kg (276 lb.), with an upper arm of 46.5 cm (18 in.), waist 1.25 m (49 in.), thigh 68 cm (27 in.) and calf 50 cm (20 in.), he provoked the wonder of Siebert, the recognized master of German weightlifting.

His progression was gradual, with his tenacious work made mostly on the premises of his shop. He got his first good result in the German Championships of 1903 when he placed third. After that, he engaged in a stiff rivalry with Andreas Maier for German leadership. While Selos didn't have great performances in the one-hand exercises and in the snatch, he became a true specialist in the two-hand events. In fact, he had exceeded 150 kg, the limit of excellence at that time for continental jerk, and on 30 July 1904 he lifted 156 kg. He then made 157 kg, followed by 159.5 kg on 16 August, but the record was not supervised by an official jury and thus not accepted.

> WHILE SELOS DIDN'T HAVE GREAT PERFORMANCES IN THE ONE-HAND EXERCISES AND IN THE SNATCH, HE BECAME A TRUE SPECIALIST IN THE TWO-HAND EVENTS.

In 1905, Selos decided to participate in the World Championships of Duisburg. During that time, Steinbach and the other Austrian, Witzelsberger, had exceeded the lifts of Türk. Finally, on 6 May, Selos performed a new German record in the two-hand jerk with 159.25 kg, surpassing the older Beck's limit of 157.5 kg. In Duisburg, the Austrians confirmed their leadership and Selos placed third—his weakness in the one-hand exercises penalised him conspicuously. In order to take care of his job,

Selos did not compete much again in big competitions, but rather trained to beat the records of two-hand tests.

He frequently asked the German Federation to send officials to confirm his one-man attempts. Often his main rival Andreas Maier came to him or both of them visited the premises of the wrestling champion Franz Blonner, another big Munich centre for strength.

Selos succeeded in improving his record again in 1905. On 7 October he pressed 141.5 kg and jerked 164 kg, but again the lack of officials present penalised his efforts. On 25 October, the Federation was able to make official his lift of 162.6 kg in the two-hand jerk. Later that year he exceeded once again with 160 kg, a demonstration of his consistency.

On 5 January 1906, Selos decided to accept the challenge of Steinbach in Vienna, but he lifted only 155 kg against the 170 kg of his formidable opponent. On 8 July, he jerked again over 160 kg and finally in early August, he took the press record, performing 138 kg and surpassing the older record of Hammel by .5 kg.

On 19 February 1907, Selos conquered another record that was traditionally well-loved by the Germans: the lifting of the beer barrel. He lifted 83 litres against the 81 elevated by Beck. Later that year, Selos tried to improve this record to 90 litres, but he failed with his two attempts. However in 1907 he did reach the peak of his career. On 13 July, he advanced the jerk record to 165.75 kg and on 21 August, the press record to 140 kg. He felt strong enough for a new challenge to the Austrians and came to Vienna for the European Championships in September, but he was beaten by another Austrian star, Grafl, and finished as runner-up. It was his last participation in an international competition. At the end of the year, he performed 148 kg in the two-hand press but, unfortunately once again, the record was not accepted.

Selos planned another effort for 1908. He varied the exercises a bit and he trained also in the correct [orthodox] style in the clean, taking the bar from the floor to the chest in one move. His clean and press of 130 kg with some back-bending were remarkable. His best two-hand jerk performance of the year was 163.5 kg. In 1909, the journal *Athletik* credited his two-hand clean and press of 115 kg in the style closer to the French orthodox move, and at the same level as the best specialists in this event. In April, he was able to elevate 118 kg in the correct style, keeping the bar overhead while standing on only one leg. Finally, he did beat the two-hand press record on 26 May with 146.25 kg.

Unfortunately, 1909 was the final great season for Selos, whose strength weakened rapidly. He died still young on 6 March 1913.

> FINALLY, HE DID BEAT THE TWO-HAND PRESS RECORD ON 26 MAY WITH 146.25 KG.

Foundations:
Shoulder Pain? Join the Club

Jon Bruney

Most guys who are in the iron game understand that discomfort is part of training. All lifters know what it's like to wake up with some aches and pains the morning after a day of intense heavy training. The pain that I will address in this article is different. I am talking about nagging discomfort that keeps you from giving your best in every workout. Training heavy can lead to tweaked shoulders and elbows. Fortunately, there is a solution to help restore, rejuvenate, and even prevent sore shoulders. That solution is club training.

I have been swinging various clubs for several years. I have clubs ranging from 2 lb. to 45 lb. Since adding a few key club-swinging exercises to my strength and conditioning regimen, my shoulders have never felt better. I have experienced increased mobility, reduced pain, and strengthening in my shoulders as a result of club training. This article will get you started with some basic club exercises that will benefit any strength and conditioning program.

Jon's selection of clubs.
JoLynn Bruney photos.

For warming up the shoulders, I like to do arm circles with light clubs. I was surprised to see how much my workouts benefited from the lighter clubs, since I was used to training with a 45-lb. club. The light clubs will lubricate your joints and prepare your shoulders for heavy pressing. I use 2-lb. clubs for the arm circles. Simply pick up a pair of light clubs and begin to do arm circles in all directions. Get creative with the movements and continue until your shoulders feel nice and warm. If you're using clubs for rehab, you will find the light clubs will increase blood flow to the shoulders.

Arm circles with a pair of 2-lb. Indian clubs.

To perform the following exercises, you start with your clubs in "order" position. Grab the clubs and swing them up to where your elbows are bent at 90 degrees and the club head is pointing straight to the ceiling. Your arms will look as if you are in the mid-range portion of a hammer curl. You will need to grasp the clubs tightly to hold them in this position. Once

Clubs in order position.

you are comfortable with the order position, you can try the exercises listed below.

The first exercise is the circle around the head. This exercise will strengthen your entire shoulder girdle. Start with two clubs in order position and take your right hand and move it diagonally toward your left shoulder, allowing the club to fall behind you. As the club is falling, bring your forearm over your head. With one fluid movement, snap your arm forward, returning the club to the order position. Repeat with the other arm. For warming up or rehabbing the shoulders, perform 10 or more reps per arm with medium-weight clubs in the 10- to 25-lb. range.

Circle around the head.

The next exercise is the swipe. To perform a swipe, swing the clubs up into order position and let the clubs fall directly behind the shoulder. This provides a tremendous stretch. Snap the arms forward and let the clubs return to order position. Once in order position, push the clubs away from the body, allowing them to swing downward. Bend your knees slightly as the clubs swing behind you. Swing the clubs forward and repeat the movement. The entire swipe should be one smooth, continuous movement.

This exercise should be done with a pair of medium weight clubs for warming up or rehab. Perform at least 15 reps. To work on strength development, use a single heavy club at 45 lb. or more, one hand at a time.

The last exercise is my personal favorite. I was first introduced to this exercise by John Brookfield about three years ago. It is called the drummer boy. John performed it for me with his giant wooden Indian clubs. This exercise feels a lot like a pullover. The drummer boy is one of the key exercises I use to train for brick breaking. To perform this exercise, swing or clean two clubs to order position; let one club fall behind the shoulder; then snap the club back into order position. Alternate between right and left arms. This exercise has a unique rhythm and feel to it and it works the entire shoulder girdle. Perform the drummer boy with a set of medium to heavy clubs. For warming up or rehab perform 10 or more reps for 2 to 5 sets.

Backward swing in the swipe.

Club exercises are a great addition to any strength athlete's routine, especially for warming up or rehabbing the shoulders. If you want to go to the next level with club training, there are many great resources available. Scott Sonnon has an entire system of club training for athletes—if you're serious about club swinging, check out his company RMAX (http://www.clubbell.tv/). Get some clubs and swing your way to strong and healthy shoulders.

Club Cal Neva Pro-Am Armwrestling Spectacular

Denise Wattles

Executive Director,
United States Armwrestling

Reno, Nevada is a place to gamble, and United States Armwrestling took a gamble of a different kind by hosting its first tournament in Reno at Club Cal Neva, and we won! Club Cal Neva proved to be the perfect location to establish an annual event. The history of the casino and hotel only adds to the prestige of the event. Club Cal Neva, built in 1962, is one of the two remaining establishments left from the original casinos built in Reno. The ambiance of this casino–hotel added to the excitement of this inaugural event.

Club Cal Neva flooded the area with information about the 1st Annual Armwrestling Spectacular, which was held October 24 and attracted a lot of new talent to the classes. It surprised me that these so-called beginner armwrestlers didn't hesitate to enter the amateur classes, bypassing the novice divisions. Eduardo and Jesus Padilla were two of the beginner armwrestlers who won amateur titles the very first time they competed in an armwrestling tournament.

It was obvious from the start of weigh-ins that the turnout would include some of the elite professionals in our sport. John Brzenk and Tom Nelson always have great matches, and to quote John, "Tom has probably beaten me more times than I have beaten him." Don't necessarily confuse that with Tom actually placing first ahead of John in a class, just that Tom has beaten him once, and John has come back to beat him twice in the finals. Regardless, these two are always exciting to watch.

I think the person I was most impressed with this weekend was Sammie Hattabaugh. At age 56, Sammie has been competing for a very

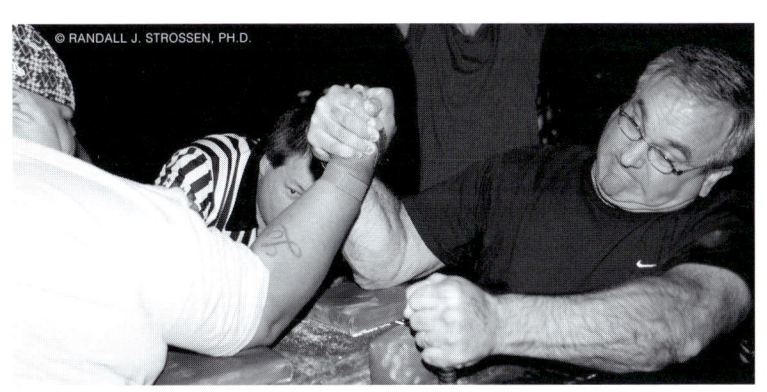

Sammie Hattabaugh (r.) goes through Marc Lowery (l.) on his way to placing "first after John." Randall J. Strossen photos.

long time. Even breaking his right arm several years ago in a match with John Parton didn't slow down his determination to come back better than ever, and he has. Every athlete in the pro right-hand 243+ class was a minimum of ten years younger than he is, and also heavier. Marc Lowery tops the scale at over 400 lb., almost twice Sammie's size, but Sammie gave him the battle of his life at the table and came away with the win. The only man who beat Sammie was John Brzenk. Placing "first after John" is something to be proud of, Sammie!

> The only man who beat Sammie was John Brzenk. Placing "first after John" is something to be proud of, Sammie!

had almost a dozen men entered, all of whom had the ability to place first. In the second round Randy Weaver handed Chris K. his first loss, dropping him to the losers' bracket. While in the losers' bracket, Chris K. had some serious battles with the others who joined him as the event continued. His teammate Vazgen had also entered this class, even though he only weighs about 140 lb., and placed a respectable fourth after several wins on the B-side. Eric Wolfe remained undefeated right-handed despite the determination and skill of Randy Weaver in his final match. Chris K. won the left-hand 198-lb. class but had to settle for a third in this division. In the heavier +243-lb. classes, Chris received a third left-handed and a fourth right-handed.

Long name—big results

Vazgen Soghoyan has secured a sponsor who is very interested in the sport and the athletes involved in armwrestling. Several men with whom Vazgen has been practicing came to this event and really shook up the classes. Khachatur Chakhmakhchyan (Chris K.), of Armenian descent, entered four divisions and placed in the top four in all of them. Left-handed, Eric Wolfe came close to beating Chris but just didn't have enough power to finish him off, settling for second place ahead of Josh Atchison and Barrett Smallwood.

Right-handed was a different story for Chris K. The pro right 177–198-lb. class

© RANDALL J. STROSSEN, PH.D.

"Chris K." (Khachatur Chakhmakhchyan) (r.) got the better of Eric Wolfe (l.) left-handed, but Eric won the 177s right, and was second to John Brzenk in the 199s right and second to Chris in the 177s left.

SMACK TALK ON MESSAGE BOARDS ENTICED OTHERS TO CHOOSE SIDES AND ANTICIPATE WHEN THESE TWO WOULD MEET AT THE TABLE.

Luke Kindt (l.) and Brandon Dye (r.): don't take your eye off the ball . . . Brandon won right-handed and Luke won left-handed.

The rivalry

Within the last year a rivalry has been developing between Brandon Dye and Luke Kindt. They have both competed in the 154-lb. division for several years, but have made the decision to quit losing weight for a class and compete at their "walking around" weight of 176 lb. Smack talk on message boards enticed others to choose sides and anticipate when these two would meet at the table. Luke and Brandon each had entered the left- and right-hand pro divisions so they would have the opportunity to prove who was better in each arm, or prove that one of them dominated the other in both arms. We wouldn't have to wait long before we would see these guys at the table—luck of the draw paired Brandon and Luke in the second round left-handed. One of them would have to make the longer journey to the finals in the losers' bracket if they were to meet again. This time Luke had the quicker start, pinning Brandon to the pad for the win.

Luke's match in the semi-finals was against Russell Jodrey, who in the past has not been able to give Luke much of a run for his money—but this time it was different. Russell is religious about working out with kettlebells and it has really paid off! Drawing Russell into a hook proved almost deadly for Luke. Luke was certainly not expecting this from the much smaller Russell. After a very strenuous

> DRAWING RUSSELL INTO A HOOK PROVED ALMOST DEADLY FOR LUKE.

match, Luke did come out the victor—but with Russell's performance, it could not be assumed that it would be Brandon and Luke in the finals. The door was definitely open for several other men, including Ulysses Jones and Jae T. Hamilton, to place in the top spot.

It was several hours and many matches before the results were determined. Brandon Dye, after dropping to the losers' bracket, lost his very next match to Darren Wartena, ending his participation left-handed. The left-handed 176-lb. competition got a lot more exciting in the finals when Russell beat Luke, handing him his first loss. They had to meet a second time to determine the champion, and when the class was finished, Luke Kindt did manage to win first place, with Russell in second, followed by Ulysses Jones and Darren Wartena in third and fourth, respectively.

Right-handed was a very different story. I didn't realize how close in talent Brandon and Luke really are because they could not be built more differently. Brandon is short and muscular while Luke is tall and lean. They also use very different techniques when they pull, Luke being a top roller and Brandon normally using a dive move. No matter what moves each used, the others in their paths right-handed weren't very successful. Only Mike McGraw and Vazgen Soghoyan were able to hang in there and ended up taking third and fourth, respectively, with Brandon winning the title and Luke as the "bridesmaid." At least this weekend, Luke was the superior armwrestler left-handed and Brandon was better right-handed. Does that mean it was a tie?

Vazgen moving up

Vazgen Soghoyan never ceases to amaze me. He holds three world titles at 132 lb. and in September he placed second at 143 lb. in Venice, Italy, at the World Championships. I can only assume that because he entered three professional right-hand divisions—154-lb., 176-lb., and 198-lb.—in this tournament, he wants to get used to pulling heavier athletes. I do know that he does not want to pull 132 lb. at the World's anymore, so it does make sense. The 154-lb. athletes do challenge him because he is so light, but he usually wins his division at that weight. I hadn't realized that he is also very competitive in the heavier classes; in fact, in addition to winning his own class, he placed fourth in both of the upper divisions. I am sure it was a shock to the men he beat at 198 lb.! It will be interesting to see how Vazgen does in upcoming tournaments in the heavier classes.

Tom vs. John

Tom Nelson had injured his right arm in a previous tournament so he entered only two left-hand classes this weekend. John Brzenk entered his usual four classes to increase his odds of taking home the most prize money. I have said it before, and it was still true this weekend, that the matches between John and Tom have more intensity at the table than any other pair of athletes. The crowd can't help but get emotionally involved when these men are up.

> . . . AND IT WAS STILL TRUE THIS WEEKEND, THAT THE MATCHES BETWEEN JOHN AND TOM HAVE MORE INTENSITY AT THE TABLE THAN ANY OTHER PAIR OF ATHLETES.

John and Tom had five matches against each other in their two classes, with Tom beating John once in the left-hand superheavyweight finals. In fact, Tom slammed John to the pad so quickly that everyone did a double take. If he could do that so decisively once, I halfway expected Tom to hit John quickly again and take home first place. However, as usual, John was more prepared the second time for Tom's hit and caught him in the middle of the table, and then slowly dropped Tom's hand to the pad for the pin. I truly think that in the U.S. Tom has the biggest chance of making an impact on our sport similar to John Brzenk. Just don't tell him that or it will go to his head!

> IN FACT, TOM SLAMMED JOHN TO THE PAD SO QUICKLY THAT EVERYONE DID A DOUBLE TAKE.

Club Cal Neva was so impressed with the skill and excitement of armwrestling that they have decided to sponsor the USAA National Armwrestling Championships starting in 2010. The USAA Nationals is celebrating its sixteenth anniversary in May and it will be fantastic to bring the event to Reno, Nevada. Reno and Club Cal Neva have so much to offer the hundreds that attend the event each year. It is easier to get to, plus Cal Neva has a free airport shuttle so it isn't necessary to rent a car. We are very excited about this move and look forward to a long and wonderful relationship with Cal Neva. See you in May 2010! **M**

1st Annual Club Cal Neva Armwrestling Spectacular 2009 – Final Results

Men's pro right

0–154	Vazgen Soghyoan/Shane Davis/Ruben DePoorter/Rickey Swann
155–176	Brandon Dye/Luke Kindt/Mike McGraw/Vazgen Soghoyan
177–198	Eric Wolfe/Randy Weaver/Chris K./Vazgen Soghoyan
199–242	John Brzenk/Eric Wolfe/Shaun Nacey/Chris K.
243+	John Brzenk/Sammie Hattabaugh/Marc Lowery/John Vandiver

Men's pro left

0–154	Shane Davis/Nicholas Williams
155–176	Luke Kindt/Russell Jodrey/Ulysses Jones/Darren Wartena
177–198	Chris K./Eric Wolfe/Josh Atchison/Barrett Smallwood
199–242	John Brzenk/Tom Nelson/Chris K./Shaun Nacey
243+	John Brzenk/Tom Nelson/John Vandiver/Marc Lowery

Three Lessons Learned from Jim Schmitz

Darryl Jarman

A few years back I found myself in the enviable position of being able to train with Jim Schmitz at Valencia Street Muscle and Fitness in San Francisco, California. I was just turning 40 years old at the time and ended up training with Jim for about a year. Jim is a very funny man to be around, and not a bad coach, either! While I had no illusions that he could turn me into a champion of any sort, I was hopeful that he could help me become stronger, get fitter, and hold off some of the effects of aging I was beginning to feel. And it turns out that is just what he did.

Jim always seemed to have a joke or story to fit any occasion, and he was never at a loss for words. One day, the air conditioning had broken in the locker room and it was feeling and smelling just as you would expect. I walked over to Jim after changing and told him it was getting close to hazardous in there. He said, "Well, I don't want you spending so much time in there that you end up falling in love!"

When it came to coaching, though, he seemed to have less to say, with only the occasional "faster, faster" or "how did that feel?" after a heavy attempt. I asked him why he was so sparing with his coaching and he said, "Most people are thinking too much as it is when they are lifting, so I don't give them any more than what is needed." The most important things I learned while training with Jim were:

1. one set to feel good
2. the Schmitz diet
3. how to progress on pull-ups

One set to feel good

Coming into training, I knew my knees would be trouble: I have had 6 knee surgeries, including two ACL replacements, and all that scar tissue was bound to cause problems at some point. I had told Jim about this the first day and he asked if I thought I could do the full Olympic lifts. I said I did not know but I wanted to try. I never was able to feel comfortable doing the full versions, but I was getting everything I wanted from the power versions. After training with Jim for 4 or 5 months and doing a lot of power snatches, power cleans, squats, and split jerks, though, my knees finally had had enough. They started asking me to stop by sending a stabbing pain every time I got into the quarter squat position to catch a power clean or was on my way down or up with a squat. That forced me to make some changes.

Jim asked me what I would like to do while I took a bit of a break from the Olympic-style lifts. I weighed about 230 lb. at 6' 2" and was about 25% body fat—not too good. I said I would like to lose some weight, work on my deadlifts (for some reason those never bothered my knees), and see if I could work up to 10 pull-ups. He thought those goals sounded like the right things to work toward, so I started doing heavy clean deadlifts and shrugs twice a week—Tuesdays and Fridays—as the only heavy work at all.

It does not take too long to work up to a heavy single or double in one lift, so that left me with time and energy for something else. That is when Jim suggested I do "one set to feel good" over on the machines in the main part of the gym. It was a play on the "one set to failure" fad that was popular at the time. "The weight does not matter. Just do the exercises until you feel good, and then stop." What, no pump, burn, failure, forced reps? It turns out that knowing when to stop was the most important thing I learned.

It seems to me that resistance training has three main applications: 1) rehabilitation from injury, 2) general fitness and conditioning, and 3) specific training for heavy sports (e.g., strongman, Highland Games, powerlifting, Olympic-style weight lifting, and bodybuilding). Rehabilitation and specific training for heavy sports involve a fair amount of pain and suffering, but general fitness and conditioning should not. I spent about 90% of my time going from machine to machine doing however many reps felt good. Usually I would not change the selected weight when I got to a machine—I would just leave it wherever it had been set by the previous user. Sometimes that meant 20 or 30 reps, sometimes it was 5 or 6 reps—but there was always a point where it felt good, and I learned that even one more rep could diminish that good feeling. If I could stop before the onset of discomfort, I found that that good feeling stayed with me. Old joint pains and muscle strains seemed to go away, and I had more energy and felt much better overall.

Looking back I can see that "one set to feel good" was the real reason that I continued to progress on all my goals—clean deadlift and shrugs, pull-ups, weight loss, and knee-pain recovery. Being and feeling healthy really is the foundation for long-term strength gains.

The Schmitz diet

I was feeling fat and slow and none too comfortable in my clothes. I had done the *SUPER SQUATS* program 3 years before and really gained a lot of strength, which was still with me. Unfortunately I had also gained body fat that was also still with me. For my age and health, I needed to lose some weight. But how would I do that and not give up the strength I had fought so hard to gain doing those darn 20-rep squats!? Jim said I could look through a sports nutrition book for some suggestions about diet or I could do the "Schmitz diet." I had read the book he suggested some years before and was not too taken with any of the diets, so I asked Jim about the Schmitz diet.

"Well, you go ahead and load up your plate just like you always do, . . . [I liked what I was hearing so far!] . . . but before you eat, take your knife and draw a line right down the middle. Then dump half of it off your plate and eat the rest." Well that sounded easy enough. "So then I just eat the

> IT TURNS OUT THAT KNOWING WHEN TO STOP WAS THE MOST IMPORTANT THING I LEARNED.

rest of it a few hours later?" I asked. "No, you don't ever eat it." Turns out the Schmitz diet is very easy to understand. And how hard could it be to follow? I did it . . . for 6 weeks. Then one weekend I could not stand it any longer. I had been hungry for so long, I started eating and did not stop. Come Tuesday I showed up at the gym to confess that I had fallen off the wagon. Jim looked at me, confused. I said, "The Schmitz diet, I've fallen off the wagon—I have been eating all I can get into my mouth for past three or four days." Jim asked, "Didn't I tell you?" "Tell me what?" I asked. "You are supposed to eat the half portions during the week, and then eat anything you want on the weekends. How long have you been doing just the half portions?" "Six weeks!" I exclaimed. Jim has a very comforting laugh! He wanted to know how I had lasted that long!

For the next 4 months I ate half portions during the week and then all I wanted during the weekends. And it worked! Jim asked me one day in April how much weight I had lost. I said, "Not much—only about 10 pounds." He said the diet was working wonderfully, and he was right. I ended up weighing about 210 lb. with 12% body fat. My lean bodyweight increased from 172 lb. to 185 lb., a gain of 13 lb. of muscle and a loss of 33 lb. of fat! My strength had improved as well—the clean deadlift and shrugs went up by 15%, and I made my pull-up goal. In other words, I had gained muscle and strength and lost body fat on a reduced-calorie diet while doing heavy training and feeling hungry almost all the time. Turns out that hunger might not be as reliable a guide to what your body needs as you think!

> TURNS OUT THAT HUNGER MIGHT NOT BE AS RELIABLE A GUIDE TO WHAT YOUR BODY NEEDS AS YOU THINK!

One more bit of advice. I came in to train one day and complained to Jim that I was feeling hungry all the time and did not know how much longer I could last. I was hoping he would give me permission to eat a bit more, but no, no, no—no sympathy, no extra food, no more complaints! He did give me permission to drink more; however, it was not what I had hoped for—a protein shake or some such—just more water. The idea was to get some feeling of fullness in my stomach. And that trick works too, by the way. Drinking when you are hungry, giving it some time to help you feel a bit full before you eat, can help you eat less.

I must say, however, that after 3 months or so of being on the Schmitz diet I lost track of what half of my "normal" amount of food was. I could not keep cutting things in half. You know, is this half of the normal plate or half of half of what is now my new normal plate? I solved this by getting a bit more structured: five small meals a day about three hours apart with 20 grams of protein in each and 300-400 calories. I was still hungry, but these small meals were just enough to take the edge off the hunger and give me all the protein I needed. After finishing I would tell myself, only 3 hours and I can take the edge off again. We can endure anything for 3 hours!

I found that on Friday nights I would be nearly dying for what became my favorite Saturday morning breakfast—powdered milk-fortified pancakes with peanut butter and lots of maple syrup. But the funny thing was it began taking less and less of this to fill me up. I started with 6 or more plate-sized pancakes and maybe 2 cups of peanut butter, but afer a while I felt stuffed with 2 cakes and a few knifefuls of peanut butter. And to top it off, that one "huge" meal lasted me almost all day. So in reality, even on the full eating days I was eating less. Make no mistake though, coming down from the weekend food high made Mondays the hardest day of the week!

Pull-up progress

The pull-up program was simple and, like all of Jim's advice, worked perfectly. I was going to the gym on Tuesdays and Fridays. Jim said, "After you are warmed-up, do as many pull-ups as you can. Then go over to the assisted pull-up machine, take off about 100 pounds and do 10 pull-ups—that's it." I did as told and here is what I found. On the first Tuesday I did 3 pull-ups and then did my assisted 10. But come Friday, I could only do 2 pull-ups. What? I thought this was supposed to increase the number I could do! Oh, well, let's see what happens next week. Next Tuesday I did 4 pull-ups. Maybe this will work after all, oh ye of little faith in Jim. Friday came along, though, and I was back down to 2—and that is the way it went. Tuesday I would increase a pull-up or 2 and Friday I would lose a pull-up or 2. In about 6 weeks I was doing my 10 pull-ups on Jim's special wide-grip handles attached to the power rack, but only on Tuesdays; Fridays I did more like 6 or 7. Then I started adding weight to see if I could do 10 at my old weight of 230 lb. And I could! Just to keep it fun, Jim would challenge me to pull-ups every Friday. At first he had me, then we tied, and finally I passed him! And like the great coach Jim is, he was happy for me when I did.

All this—one set to feel good; the Schmitz diet; and heavy clean deadlift and shrugs and pull-ups—lasted about 5 months. My knees were feeling better and I wanted to get back to the power Olympic-style lifts. Also, I knew both Jim's time at Valencia Muscle and Fitness and my time at the San Francisco job were drawing to a close. After starting back light to see how the knees felt, I began adding weight and within 3 weeks I was power snatching 15% more than my best ever, and my power clean and jerk had stayed the same but felt more solid.

All in all it was the best year of lifting I have ever had. I lost fat, gained muscle and strength, held off aging for a bit longer, and enjoyed the company of one great coach and an even greater person—Jim Schmitz. M

> AT FIRST HE HAD ME, THEN WE TIED, AND FINALLY I PASSED HIM!

Customize Your Program to Fit Your Individual Needs

Bill Starr

Author of *The Strongest Shall Survive: Strength Training for Football* and *Defying Gravity*

When I moved from Marion, Indiana, to York, Pennsylvania in February 1966 to become Tommy Suggs' assistant editor at *Strength & Health* magazine, I was stoked. Now I would be able to find out the York Barbell secret—that magic formula that made the York lifters champions. I had visited the York Barbell Club (YBC) on several occasions, but now I would have the opportunity to watch the training sessions and be able to ask the necessary questions in order to find the "secret."

In the ensuing months, I closely observed everything that Homer Brannum, Tony Garcy, Bill March, Bob Bednarski, and Tommy Suggs did during their training sessions. And because the YBC was such a magnet for Olympic weightlifting, I also got to watch many other champions train: Bob Bartholomew and Gerald Moyer from Allentown, Ernie Pickett and Barry Whitcomb from Maryland, Frank Capsouras from New Jersey, and Joe Puleo and Norb Schemansky from Detroit.

> WHAT I WAS SEEKING WAS THE SAME THING EVERY OTHER ASPIRING OLYMPIC LIFTER WAS LOOKING FOR . . .

What I was seeking was the same thing every other aspiring Olympic lifter was looking for—a cut-and-dried formula for success in the sport, a routine laid out precisely with a specific number of sets and reps with the exact poundage for the best exercises, plus duration of training and how often to train in a week.

What I was seeing at YBC, however, only confused me. To my surprise, each lifter trained differently—not just a bit differently here and there, but often almost exactly the opposite of another national champion. What really stunned me was that nearly every one of them would alter their routines midway through their workouts. I had been trained by Sid Henry—he was a strict disciplinarian and every lifter did the exact same routine. Variations were not allowed. This was ideal for a beginner like me, but these guys weren't beginners and made all kinds of changes in their intended workouts.

Tony Garcy was the exception—he never varied from his well-planned sessions for that week, regardless. Everyone else, however, did. Bednarski might plan on going heavy on his presses on Monday, and then when he discovered that he had not fully recovered from his heavy workout on Saturday, he'd pull back and do three or four sets of light singles. March was also very flexible. If things weren't going right on the quick lifts, he'd abandon them and do back squats or work in the power rack. Suggs would also throw away his intended workout and just do isotonic-isometric movements in the rack. At one session, Homer power cleaned three sets, declared, "It's not right," and left the gym. This was unheard of. I could understand making changes when it was obvious a lifter wasn't on his game that day, but to quit altogether? However, it worked for Homer.

Equally as confusing was the fact that everyone seemed to do a different assortment of exercises, even though they were all training for the exact same sport. Bednarski only did the three competitive lifts—press, snatch, and clean and jerk—along with back squats. March often just worked out in the power rack and totaled on Saturdays. Suggs and Garcy had more variety in their routines, adding steep inclines, high pulls, shrugs, and good mornings. But even when the exercises were the same, the manner in which they did them usually differed. Garcy did his good mornings with his legs straight like the Europeans, while Suggs preferred doing them with knees slightly bent, to take the stress off the hamstrings.

> AT ONE SESSION, HOMER POWER CLEANED THREE SETS, DECLARED, "IT'S NOT RIGHT," AND LEFT THE GYM. THIS WAS UNHEARD OF.

Some trained just three days a week, some four, and Garcy put in six sessions a week, including two a day twice a week. Garcy's sessions were also quite long and his workload was enormous. Bednarski seldom did more than two exercises at a workout and then only a few sets for lower reps. Garcy moved through his lifts in a quick fashion while Bednarski and March lingered between attempts.

I had been hoping to find a pattern that I could use for my own training, but all that I had found was . . . there was not a pattern. Nor was there any resemblance in their technique. Pickett and Knipp seemed to merely overpower the weights, as did Bartholomew. Moyer, Garcy, and Capsouras utilized hairline form and quickness. All had a slightly different way of pressing and jerking, Knipp split snatched, as I did, while the rest employed the squat style. Some power cleaned for their presses; others full cleaned.

I knew before moving to York that there wasn't a coach for the lifters, a truth that Hoffman did not reveal as he wanted everyone in the Olympic lifting community to believe that he attended all the workouts and carefully laid out training schedules for his athletes. For a short time, I thought he just might be too busy to come to the gym and give pointers to the lifters, and then I found out that he didn't know the first thing about coaching.

Dick "Smitty" Smith was always in attendance, but his role as a motivator was not the same as having a real coach, like the great Hungarian lifter

Mihaly Huszka, who would soon take over that position at the Duncan YMCA in Chicago.

It was clear that the lifters who trained regularly at the YBC and those who showed up during the week or on Saturdays were totally in charge of their own destinies. Once I took the time to stop and look at the situation, I determined that it made perfect sense. Each of these athletes started training on their own. Some, like me, were fortunate enough to come across a capable coach, but most did not, so they were very much at ease in designing their own routines and making adjustments when they deemed necessary. Had they been assigned to a coach, most would have balked at doing what someone else told them to do. They were experienced and completely comfortable with their own counsel, which was very rational because who can understand how a certain exercise feels better than the person performing it? No one.

After several months of taking notes, talking with the lifters and watching them train, I still had no clue from what I heard or saw as to how to put together my own program, other than the one I was already using. However, after pondering the matter a bit longer, I started figuring out some key points.

First, every lifter was constantly trying to improve a weaker exercise. They never allowed a weak area to fall so far behind that it ended up affecting their total. The weak lift was given priority until it was pulled up and then another was put up front in the workouts.

> HAD THEY BEEN ASSIGNED TO A COACH, MOST WOULD HAVE BALKED AT DOING WHAT SOMEONE ELSE TOLD THEM TO DO.

Second, they never did exercises that they didn't think would help them in a direct manner. That's why most just stuck with the basics: pressing, snatching, clean and jerking, and back squats. Some liked to build a lot of variety into their routines, others didn't. Those who knew that they couldn't handle a huge workload did shorter sessions.

These lifters were basically using instinctive training, since that's what got them to their current strength level. Intuitive or instinctive training isn't in vogue in the twenty-first century. Those interested in strength training want to be told exactly what to do, how long to do it, and how much weight to use on the specific movements in the program. Just put in the effort and the results will come, no thinking involved.

I really have no problem with this at the beginner's level. I start all my athletes on a very regimented schedule, with all the sets, reps, and numbers in place—all they have to do is follow the map. This is useful because it helps the athletes learn proper technique on the various movements and allows them to establish a solid strength foundation. It's like learning basic math before moving on to algebra, trigonometry, and calculus.

Yet even at this stage, I still make sure that I am conscious of individual differences. This is a prime consideration in every program, from the very beginner to the extremely advanced. Even though a score of athletes are all learning the exact same routine, there will be many variations on how they perform the exercises. Levers play a big role, as does the ability to focus on the task at hand, prior experience, body size, and of course, athletic ability. Also to be considered are the athlete's capacity to recover from a strenuous session, and his diet and rest patterns.

An athlete, or group of athletes, has to be closely observed in order to notice any problems that may occur while perfecting technique on the selected exercises. The power clean is one of my primary movements for any athlete, male or female. The majority learned the correct form rather easily, but there always seemed to be one or two on every sports team who struggled with this lift. I had a male basketball player who could not break the habit of bending his arms way too soon. I worked with him until I became frustrated, and then checked myself. The purpose behind doing the power clean was not so much to establish absolutely perfect form, but rather to help him get stronger in the back and legs. Perfect form helps, but it isn't essential. I told him to continue to do the lift the best he could and try to improve the numbers. It turned out that once he started using some taxing poundage, his form flaw disappeared almost completely.

The struggle with the lifter's form reminded me that some of the best Olympic lifters in the country had flagrant form mistakes in their pulls. Norb Schemansky was my first hero in the sport. I still consider him one of the greatest ever to mount a lifting platform. I saw him lift at the 1964 Nationals and again at the Olympic Trials at the New York World's Fair that same year. I recall two things: his massive physique, which exuded pure power, and that he bent his arms too soon in the snatch and clean. That is, too soon according to every authority I'd ever talked to, but not for him. Somehow he figured out how to utilize the early bending of his arms to his advantage. His 363-lb. (165-kg) split snatch was the proof of the pudding.

> I RECALLED TWO THINGS: HIS MASSIVE PHYSIQUE, WHICH EXUDED PURE POWER, AND THAT HE BENT HIS ARMS TOO SOON IN THE SNATCH AND CLEAN.

Another who bent his arms ridiculously early was Mario Martinez. The first time I saw him clean, I thought, he must be kidding. The start resembled a bent-over row. Later, I got to regularly watch him train at Jim Schmitz's Sports Palace in San Francisco. The pull to his waist was so unorthodox it seemed that it would be impossible for him to finish the clean. But once the bar reached that height, everything changed. His torso shot upright, his arms became straight, the bar was tucked in close to his body, and he was suddenly in perfect position to provide a powerful finish to the clean.

While I'm not advocating that anyone use faulty form, there is no doubt that in some cases it's effective. The main point I am making in this piece is that we're all individuals, and what may work for 99% of the people who lift weights may not work for you. Conversely, a certain style that is totally

> CONVERSELY, A CERTAIN STYLE THAT IS TOTALLY INCORRECT FOR THAT SAME PERCENTAGE OF LIFTERS MAY BE PERFECT FOR YOU.

Mario Martinez (USA), who characteristically pulled with bent arms, was an Olympic silver medalist (and fourth in another Olympics). He was also the first American to both snatch over 400 lb. and clean and jerk over 500 lb.—and he did it in the same contest.
Randall J. Strossen photo.

incorrect for that same percentage of lifters may be perfect for you.

Everyone is well aware that individuals differ—just look at a set of siblings in any family and you'll see a wide range of skin, eye, and hair color. One brother is tall and built like a tank; his younger brother is almost frail, yet they share the same genes. I knew that people were diverse in many regards from an early age, but it wasn't until I read *You Are Extraordinary* by Roger Williams for an assignment in a sociology class in college that I learned just how different one person is from another. In his opening remarks Williams states, "There is no average person. We as individuals cannot be averaged with other people. Inborn individuality is a highly significant factor in all our lives—as inescapable as the fact that we are human."

He was not just talking about appearance or mannerisms. He also pointed out how different we are internally. As an example, he uses the stomach. We all have them and know their general shape, location, and function. Right? Not really. There are as many as nine different positions of the stomach, ranging from being almost entirely up in the chest—from the breastbone up—to far down in the abdomen. A Mayo Clinic study of the gastric juices of about five thousand people who had no known stomach ailments showed that the juices varied at least a thousand-fold in the pepsin content.

Add to the many variations in the size and functions of all our organs, the psychological factors such as temperament, ability to cope with stress, current mental and physical health, occupation, family involvement or lack thereof, financial state, age, and so on, and it's easy to understand that if a person wants to continue to make improvements in his weight training he has to take all these variables into account.

That's what the York lifters were doing, although I seriously doubt if any of them could have explained why they followed a certain program and avoided some exercises that others liked. They did follow certain principles, knowingly or unknowingly, such as the heavy, light, and medium system [for more information, see "Utilizing the Heavy, Light, and Medium Concept" by Bill Starr, *MILO*, September 2009, Vol. 17, No. 2]. Sid Henry had taught me how to utilize it and it was a regimented part of every weekly routine. Garcy

> HE ALSO POINTED OUT HOW DIFFERENT WE ARE INTERNALLY. THERE ARE AS MANY AS NINE DIFFERENT POSITIONS OF THE STOMACH . . .

was also adamant about having it in a strict place during the week. Others weren't nearly as structured; they were much more flexible in their approaches. Bednarski and March were particularly good at this. They might be planning on going light on a certain exercise, but once they got into the workout and they found that everything was clicking, they scrapped the light session and went after the heavier poundage. In the same vein, a short session might have evolved into a long one when they knew they were on that day. Then they would come back the next time and take a less demanding workout. They didn't so much plan this out, but just felt it was the right approach.

As I mentioned, these lifters gave priority to the weaker areas and this is a key principle for anyone at any strength level. Plus, they primarily did movements for the major groups: shoulder girdle, back, and hips/legs. I was one of the few who bothered at all with the smaller groups. I systematically worked my abs, lumbars, and calves, since I believed they played important roles in elevating heavy weights overhead.

Another aspect of training that they understood about themselves was how much of a workload they could carry. After I moved from the 181-lb. class to the 198-lb. class, I found that I could handle a much greater volume of work and still be able to recover. The extra 20 lb. and all the protein powder I could ingest were the main reasons for this. I was constantly trying to do more and more work to increase my overall strength base and it was working, although I did fall into the overtraining trap a few times. But in my mind, the only way to know if you're doing too much is to overtrain and then quickly recognize this state and pull back.

When I arrived at York, Suggs was rehabbing his knees and wasn't doing any heavy lifting. After much therapy and advice from Dr. Russell Wright, the team physician for all of Detroit's pro teams, he was able to resume a schedule of hard training for the Olympic lifts. We started training together since we were fairly close in most of the lifts. After a short time he realized that what was working for me was detrimental for him. We continued to train together using the exact same program, but he did half as much total work as I did in a session. It would seem that since I was able to work longer and use a greater workload that I would end up making much bigger lifts. This didn't happen. Our improvement was nearly identical, and at the end of our respective careers, we had both posted the same best total of 1035 lb.; and in addition, our best on the press, snatch, and clean and jerk were only pounds apart.

Tommy understood his strengths and limitations and was smart enough to do what was best for him. Had he staunchly tried to stay with my concept of training, he would not have made the same gains he did and most likely would have sustained an injury. Had I decided to alter my planned schedule and follow his abbreviated program, my lifts would have suffered. I know this because I gave it a try for a week.

This is why any article in a magazine or a program outlined in a book has to be considered from an individual standpoint. While it may work nicely for everyone around you, it may be a flop for you. A program that brings results for your training mate may not be right for you. As I said above, a set formula-type routine will almost always make you stronger in the beginning, but once you move into the intermediate and advanced levels, you have to start utilizing the concept of individual differences and design a routine that fits you.

> AFTER A SHORT TIME HE REALIZED THAT WHAT WAS WORKING FOR ME WAS DETRIMENTAL FOR HIM.

There is a longstanding truism in strength training that the very best program is the one that produces results. The reason why most people have trouble applying that basic concept to their own training is they do not believe in their own ability to design a workable program for themselves so they turn to outside experts. There's nothing wrong with that—if there were, I'd be out of a job. But the information given out by the experts has to be filtered through your personal needs and limitations.

No one—not your wife, your best friend, or your doctor—knows your body as well as you do. No one else knows that when you try to bench press heavy weight, your right shoulder hurts severely for days after the workout. Yet, you can overhead press and incline hard and heavy with no problem. That's enough to tell you

> THERE IS A LONG-STANDING TRUISM IN STRENGTH TRAINING THAT THE VERY BEST PROGRAM IS THE ONE THAT PRODUCES RESULTS.

which exercise to tell you which exercise to omit and which to include.

Only you know that you feel better and stronger when you do five or six short sessions in a week rather than the conventional three. Or that when you attempt to expand your workload by adding in another day, you regress. Or that deadlifting with the sumo style allows you to handle much more weight than when you place your feet close together.

The fundamental lesson here is those who made it to the top in Olympic weightlifting learned to understand their individual differences and utilized that information to help them steadily improve. This is also true for just about any other athlete who excels in his or her sport, and it is exactly what everyone must do if he or she wants to stay strong and healthy.

"How do I go about this?" you are probably wondering. First of all, you already have a vast storehouse of information about yourself. For example, you know what exercises you can do that cause no pain—not the kind of pain associated with effort, but the kind where you know you're doing damage. You know how much load you can carry and what feels right as to the number of days a week you can train. You also understand what diet fits you and what supplements are beneficial and how much rest you need in order to have a productive workout.

Gather information. Some of it may be pure junk, but read that too. Filter the various views presented by different writers and determine which are valid for your situation. Discount nothing and examine everything in the context of your individual needs.

Use trial and error to determine what works and what doesn't—that's really the only way to create a program that fits you perfectly. This is the reason it takes many years to come up with a workable routine. There's no other way, unless you happen to have a coach who understands you as well as you do. There are probably five people in the country who fit this category. And while you're testing various exercises, set and rep formulas, and different routines, keep an accurate record of what transpires during those times. This will prove to be very helpful farther down the road.

This is an ongoing, never-ending process, since your needs and limitations are constantly in flux as you grow older. What was an ideal training program for you when you were in your twenties and thirties no longer brings the desired results in your forties and early fifties. The same thing happens in your late fifties and sixties. This means you have to make changes continuously if you want to stay strong and physically fit. Some find this very frustrating and extremely unfair. I simply call it a fact of life where the only constant is change. **M**

> USE TRIAL AND ERROR TO DETERMINE WHAT WORKS AND WHAT DOESN'T—THAT'S REALLY THE ONLY WAY TO CREATE A PROGRAM THAT FITS YOU PERFECTLY.

> SOME FIND THIS VERY FRUSTRATING AND EXTREMELY UNFAIR. I SIMPLY CALL IT A FACT OF LIFE . . .

Standing Weight-Over-Bar:
A Primer Course
Thom Van Vleck

If the clean and jerk is the king of lifts, then the weight-over-bar may be the king of Highland Games throws. The weight-over-bar (WOB), also known as the weight-for-height (WFH), is usually the last athletic event in the Scottish Highland Games heavy events. It is the event that often decides the overall winners and losers for the day, and it is the event that needs no judge to tell the crowd if the toss is good or not. It also showcases who might possibly be the strongest man or woman on the field, as it is the event that seemingly requires the least technique and the most explosive power.

There is a rift in the Highland Games world over this event and how it should be performed. Is the event done by standing only or can the thrower take a spin to build momentum into the toss? What about the sling from the side in a standing position? I won't try to solve that controversy and I'm not sure anyone can. This article is for the purists—it will focus on the standing throw and save the other techniques for another day.

> IT IS THE EVENT THAT OFTEN DECIDES THE OVERALL WINNERS AND LOSERS FOR THE DAY . . .

While there are many rule books from just as many organizations, they agree on the basic premise that the athlete tosses the weight with one hand over a crossbar for height. There are three attempts at each height with three misses resulting in elimination. After that, variations can result.

First, let's look at the basic rules of the toss. I say *toss* because it is said that when you throw, you are going for distance and when you toss, you are going for height. The WOB requires the athlete to toss a weight over a crossbar for height, with the greatest height winning. The weights can be of many shapes but are not to be over 18" long and are typically 12–15" long, with a handle that is grasped with one hand only.

Weights used in the WOB

Men	56 lb.
Masters men	42 lb.
Lightweights (190 lb. and under)	42 lb.
Women	28 lb.
Masters women 50 and over	20 lb.

The standards (the apparatus which the weight is tossed over) can be various widths and may employ a fixed bar or a knock-off bar. The knock-off bar is similar to your typical high jump or pole vault bar—it can be knocked off, resulting in the throw not counting. The fixed bar is, to various degrees, fixed to the uprights so that it cannot be knocked off.

Let's take a look at some of the all-time best weight-over-bar tosses from the standing position. I have researched this as best I can, but I may have missed someone and better throws are being recorded all the time. However, it will give you a good idea of what a world-class WOB height is.

All-time best weight-over-bar (traditional stand) tosses—56-lb. weight

Mike Zolkiewicz	18' 9"
Wout Zijlstra	18' 8.4"
Samundur Samundsson	18' 5"
Ben Plucknett	18' 3.5"
Bill Kazmaier	18' 3"
Matt Sandford	18'
Paul Ferency	17' 7"
Steve Santoli (amateur record)	17' 6"
Doug McDonald (Canadian record)	17' 6"
Jim McGoldrick	17' 3"

It is interesting to note that only a handful of men have cleared 18' standing, while there have been a couple of dozen at the 17' mark. The best women's toss with the 28-lb. weight (standing) belongs to Shannon Hartnett at 18' 8". The best masters' toss with the 42-lb. weight belongs to Don Stewart at 20' 6". Don is in a class by himself in this event—the second-best standing throw is at 19' and is shared by American Myles Wetzel, Scotsman Jamie Barr, and Canadian Berle Conrad.

Before you feel a little beleaguered regarding your own WOB performances, let's talk about what a good toss might be. A winning pro throw in any given meet would be in the 15'–16' range. A winning amateur mark would be 13'–14', with a good throw for a beginner at 12' or less. I recall that the amateur record when I started throwing in 1994 was just a shade over 14'. It would be a daunting task to join the above list of Highland titans!

Technique

I started this article with the statement that the weight-over-bar seemingly had the least technique of all the Highland Games heavy events. It might appear to the casual observer that a strong back and good grip are all that would be required to toss a 56-lb. weight a decent height. While those two things are keys to a good toss, they will only get you so far . . . or high, as the case may be.

Stance

The first thing you need to do is to get in the proper stance. Typically, you want the weight to swing between the legs, so you want a stance that is wide enough to allow the weight to pass through, and you want to be squared up under the bar so the weight travels up and over your head and then over the bar. Sean Betz, 2008 world champion and former world-record holder in the spin-style WOB, advised me that you want your stance as close as possible to make your release point as high as possible, but wide enough you don't tense up worrying about taking the weight in the shins.

Grip

The next thing you will do is grip the weight. Implements come in many shapes and with many types of handles: there are "D" handles (shaped like a "D") and triangles, for example, but rings seem to be the most common. Here is where you need to set your ego aside—you may be certified on a No. 3 Captains of Crush Gripper, but you will want to use a hook grip for the WOB. The reason is the same as why the Olympic lifters use the hook grip—you want your arm to stay relaxed. Sean Betz told me that he added a foot to his WOB toss by using the hook grip. The hook grip is basically wrapping your fingers over your thumb on the handle rather than the other way around. I would also advise a tacky spray or some other sticky substance to allow you to grip the ring as loosely as possible. Most athletes keep the grip overhand, but some will turn the hand at a 90-degree angle to the body with the palm facing in. Experiment to determine which works best for you.

Swing
Pick up the weight and begin to swing it between the legs like a pendulum. Don't waste energy with a lot of swings, but use the swings to get in a good position. Let your arm swing long, keep your upper body as relaxed as possible, and let the weight go underneath you, keeping your legs slightly bent with your shoulders out over your toes. You want to straighten the legs on the back swing and then bend the knees as the weight gets to then ankles, creating a stretch reflex.

Pull
I have often been told that the WOB is much like doing a weighted standing vertical jump. Ideally, you would do one swing and pull, but when you feel ready, start your final pull. As that weight gets to the ankle, you want to react with an explosive jump. You want to be quick and not too deep—it is all about hip drive, as in the second pull in a good power clean. Drive the hips! Your pull should be straight and should feel natural.

Finish
Again, I'll reference the standing vertical jump. You want to drive the hips all the way through, snap the head and shoulders back, and push on the ground as long as possible, driving up on your toes and reaching as high as possible. Build momentum at the release and explode. I like to pretend I'm trying to jump after the weight.

> SEAN BETZ TOLD ME THAT HE ADDED A FOOT TO HIS WOB TOSS BY USING THE HOOK GRIP.

It is also interesting to note that it's never too late to reinvent something. Mike Zolkiewicz recently went on a roll, eventually breaking the WOB standing world record with a toss of 18' 9". Sean Betz was on hand to see it and noted that Mike tends to come out of the swing at an angle. Whether this particular style may just suit his anatomy better, or there's something more to it (Sean theorized it gave him a slightly higher release point and more distance to apply force to the weight), it does make the point that you should experiment and find what works best for you. These pointers on technique should be guidelines at best.

Practicing the WOB
Interestingly, if you talk to most pro throwers, they spend very little time training the WOB. But don't be fooled by this—they don't train it as much for several reasons. First, most top throwers have done the WOB for years and have their technique down and only need a few throws to get in the groove. Second, there is much more to be

gained by training the other events. Al Myers, a top pro in the 1990s and perhaps the only man to ever clear 15' standing left- and right-handed in competition (after tearing his biceps), told me that he knew he was good for 15' every time, but 16' always eluded him. On the other hand, he could practice on, say, the weight-for-distance, and it might net him several feet in his competition throws. For new throwers, practicing the WOB is a must!

First, you need to have something to throw over. I recall early in my career throwing over tree branches in my yard. It doesn't matter how high you toss the weight if it doesn't go over. You want to be able to hit a height 6 times in a row in practice and when you can, that will be a good opening height. Also, check to see if a knock-off bar is being used and if it is, open a foot lower. It is better to take an extra throw at a lower height than to find yourself with a no height (NH) on the score card and in last place.

Your goals in practice should be to perfect your technique, not to break a personal record on every throw. This can be taxing on the body and there are too many events to burn all your energy on one event. Practice should be focused on developing a natural pull and increasing speed. Sean Betz thinks that you should end with a height you can barely clear, but clear it cleanly and consistently. He believes this builds confidence.

There are a lot of theories out there on using overweight and underweight implements. Some like to practice with an overweight implement so the competition weight will seem light. Some like to use an underweight implement to develop speed. I like both, but I would recommend going up or down only 2% or less. Any more will hurt your technique.

Strategies in WOB competition

The first thing you will want to do in a competition is ask the judge what rules are in effect. Some allow passes without penalty and some do a count-back to break ties. Ask the judge to brief you. At most contests, the judge's ruling is usually final: regardless of what rules the meet is running on, ask the judge how he or she interprets them. You don't want to lose because of a strategic mistake.

Most Games will employ a point system whereby first place gets 1 point, second place gets 2 points, and so on. If there are 10 to 12 athletes, you don't have to be a math wizard to figure out that a last-place finish vs. a middle-of-the-pack finish in an event can mean the difference between an overall first and finishing off the podium. I like to start at a height well below my best, usually one I will clear by 2' to 4'. First, you ensure that you don't get a no-height calling. This is automatically a last place in most cases and will kill you on points. The lower heights become my warm-ups as I dial in on greater heights, and I build confidence in my throws, which keeps me loose. Too often, especially when a knock-off bar is employed, I've seen a superior athlete come in too high and get an NH, which costs him not only the event, but the overall contest as well.

> YOUR GOALS IN PRACTICE SHOULD BE TO PERFECT YOUR TECHNIQUE, NOT TO BREAK A PERSONAL RECORD ON EVERY THROW.

Mike Zolkiewicz sets an American record of 18' 5" in the standing WOB at the 2009 Kansas City Games.
Larry Ventress, Pioneer Photography photo.

Don Stewart at age 40 throwing a 56-lb. weight over bar.
Courtesy of Don Stewart

Aaron Neighbour winning the WOB at the 2009 IHGF World Heavy Events Championships, Edinburgh, Scotland.
Thom Van Vleck photo.

Keep track of who misses. WOB events often end with multiple throwers at the same height and the countbacks are important. Most rule books require that the bar go up a minimum height, usually 1' at a time until the number of competitors dwindles to 5 or fewer. Then, the judge will usually ask the athletes what they want to go to. If you have the fewest misses, it would be in your best interest to jump up as high as possible, as you hold the tie-breaker. Of course, the opposite is true if you have the most misses.

Keep on top of it and make sure you know what the judge is going to do. Judges' decisions often are final and may not always follow the rule book. In my many years at the Games, I've seen some strange things happen, and since the WOB is often last and time is running out, judges sometimes make some odd calls in the interest of moving the event along. Knowledge is your best friend.

Weight room training for the WOB

I have observed a lot of really strong guys humbled by the WOB over the years, and I've seen guys who don't look that strong do really well with it. Obviously being as strong as possible is important in WOB success, but why do some fail and other succeed?

First, guys who are really strong in their upper bodies—maybe they are powerlifters or strongman competitors, or like my buddy Mitch Ridout, gifted with strong shoulders—fall back on that shoulder strength when doing the WOB. They often look as if they are trying to start a lawn mower—and maybe do fairly well with it because they can bench 600 lb. without a bench shirt. But ultimately, your upper body is no match for the power down below.

Second, pulling with your shoulders will tense you up and shorten your stroke. Back to the hook grip, you want to be long by staying loose in your lever (upper body) and strong in your fulcrum (posterior chain).

The biggest factor in creating WOB power is developing the posterior chain. The hamstrings, glutes, and lower back are key. Your basic squat and deadlift variations are always a good foundation, but you want to develop explosive power. This means a healthy diet of power cleans, high pulls and snatches, as well as from the hang position. Sean Betz told me he favors the hang position on cleans and snatches as they mimic the WOB better. Doing these with dumbbells and kettlebells are also a plus. Variation is important to keep things fresh. For Don Stewart, the way to figure out how well a lift will transfer to the WOB is to ask yourself if it allows you to generate great speed and reaction at the bottom with a heavy object from a static foot position.

> I HAVE OBSERVED A LOT OF REALLY STRONG GUYS HUMBLED BY THE WOB OVER THE YEARS . . .

> TOO OFTEN THROWERS JUST LIFT WEIGHTS IN THE GYM WHEN THEY NEED TO BE DOING SO MUCH MORE.

Explosive–reactive exercises are just as important. Too often throwers just lift weights in the gym when they need to be doing so much more. Plyometrics, short sprints, and medicine ball throwing are all part of a good training program for the WOB—they make you quick and athletic.

You will want to break your training into two basic phases, with the assumption that you will be training other events at the same time: 1) in-season training, which should be focused mostly on practicing the events and recuperating properly for contests; and 2) off-season training where training-hall work takes precedence and things get heavier.

Don Stewart has used two basic movements in the off-season to generate world records in the WOB in three age groups: the good morning squat (GMS) and the hang snatch-grip deadlift (HSGDL), which is a deadlift with a snatch grip from a 4" box. Don feels that both of these movements above all others give him the ability to mimic the dynamic movement of the WOB as well as provide the specific muscle recruitment—the reactivity in the hips, lower back, glutes, and hamstrings—necessary to accelerate a weight from a stand. Don says you can't break up the movement, you need to train it as a whole, and these two movements, along with the other base strength and speed movements, develop dynamic vertical strength-speed. Don will only max out a couple of times a year with the weights, focusing instead on moving fast with a good weight, but a heavy weight nonetheless.

In season, Don likes to use the power snatch and high pull with a snatch grip. These movements are not nearly as heavy as his off-season lifts, as Don wants to ensure he stays fast. A basic in-season workout will include:

2 weeks from HG event:
high pull (snatch grip) 315 x 5, 365 x 3, 405 x 1

1 week from HG event:
power snatch working up to 220/242 x 1 with no knee bend and no press out

Afterthoughts

The standing WOB will always be a favorite Highland Games heavy event. The caber may be the signature event, but the WOB has got to be a close second. It is also becoming a popular event in both strongman and Highlander (which combine strongman and Highland Games events) contests, so knowing how to improve your weight-over-bar performance is more important than ever. I mean really, what's more fun that tossing a chunk of iron and punching a hole in the sky? M

> THE STANDING WOB WILL ALWAYS BE A FAVORITE HIGHLAND GAMES HEAVY EVENT. THE CABER MAY BE THE SIGNATURE EVENT, BUT THE WOB HAS GOT TO BE A CLOSE SECOND.

2009 U.S. Invitational Heavy Events Championships and IHGF World Hammer Championships:
Non-Stop Top-Flight Throwing

Francis Brebner
Seven-time Caber World Champion

The Pleasanton Highland Games, as they are commonly called, are run by the Caledonian Club of San Francisco, California and in 2009, it celebrated its 144th Games in succession. These Games are the host of the U.S. Invitational Heavy Events Championships, organized and run by athletic director Steve Conway (of Scottish Heavy Athletics), one of the world's top-ranking international judges.

This year's line-up of professional invitees from across the U.S. consisted of Ryan Vierra, Mike Pockoski, Daniel McKim, Sean Betz, Bert Sorin, Lucais MacKay, Harrison Bailey III, Eric Frasure, and Rusty Price. There was also a little international flavor with the presence of England's Scott Rider, one of the top contenders on the international Games circuit.

The only two U.S. athletes missing from this star-studded group were Kerry Overfelt, who has had a great run of successive victories this season, and Larry Brock, who had been suffering from a badly injured ankle since the early part of the season and unfortunately had to withdraw from Pleasanton to avoid further complications. Another athlete who had a rough start to the year was Vierra, for whom at one point it looked as if the season were over due to a severe case of gout, but he managed to get back on course with his throwing later on.

28-lb. Braemar standing putt
The first day of competition got under way with perfect weather and all athletes looking ready and eager to get into the thick of the action. The opening event was the 28-lb. Braemar standing putt, and it was Rusty Price, the 2008 world stone-putting champion, who took the early lead in the first round with 36' 6". In second position was England's Scott Rider with 36' 3", and in third, Sean Betz with 36' 3-1/2".

In the second round most athletes produced their best distances, and Betz won the first event of the competition by the narrowest of margins with a distance of 37' 11-1/2", nudging Price into second place with 37' 10-1/2". This left England's Scott Rider, who looked to be having difficulty with this awkward stone, to settle for a rather disappointing third place in his favorite event, with a putt of 37' 7".

Randall J. Strossen photos.

Bert Sorin flew out from South Carolina for this contest—maybe he pocketed a bit of jet stream along the way because he sent the light hammer sailing.

16-lb. (light) hammer

The next event with the 16-lb. hammer proved to be fascinating as the first round got underway of the 2009 IHGF World Hammer Championships. Dan McKim set the mark for the others to follow with an opening throw of 129' 9". This was surpassed by the slightest of margins by Frasure and Pockoski, who now shared the lead in the first round with the same distance of 129' 9-1/2".

In the second round, McKim cranked it up a gear to reclaim the lead with a throw of 131' 2", but this again was short-lived as Pockoski surpassed him with 133' 3". To my surprise, moving up rapidly from behind with an improvement of over 6' was Bert Sorin, who, despite having to nurse a badly swollen knee and calf, produced a distance of 129' 5-1/2".

In the final round of the hammer, I noticed that a few athletes looked off with their timing and were not as fluid as I had seen in previous World Hammer Championships. Betz was one of the athletes who was having some difficulty finding his form, but he gave his all feverishly on his last attempt to claw back some very vital points, and did so with a throw of 127' 7", moving himself up from ninth position to fifth.

However, it was Bert Sorin who captivated the audience and his fellow comrades on his last attempt: with a throw of 134' 7" he won the first leg of the IHGF World Hammer Championships. Sorin looked well pleased and rightly so, but he also knew that this was just the first round of the hammer championships and anything could still happen.

BETZ WAS ONE OF THE ATHLETES WHO WAS HAVING SOME DIFFICULTY FINDING HIS FORM, BUT HE GAVE HIS ALL FEVERISHLY ON HIS LAST ATTEMPT TO CLAW BACK SOME VERY VITAL POINTS . . .

56-lb. (heavy) weight-for-distance

The concluding event of the morning's competition was the 56-lb. weight-for-distance—an event that I knew was going to be electric, as big numbers had been thrown during the season by Betz, Frasure, and Bailey. It was a case of who could keep his composure and not let the pressure get to him, while hoping to avoid similar performances to what we had witnessed in the previous event with the 16-lb. hammer.

The first round got off to a blitzing start with Frasure ripping an opening throw of 42' 7", followed by Betz with 40' 7". But it was Bailey who stole the show with an incredible icebreaker of 44' 1".

In the second round, Frasure replied to Bailey's throw with a respectable distance of 43' 11", which was followed by Vierra's 40' 11", and Pockoski pulled out a noble distance of 41' 4". Charging from behind was Betz with a well-increased distance of 43', but again it was the cool cat Bailey who pulled it up a notch with yet another grand throw of 44' 11" to uphold his lead.

Going into the final round of the 56-lb. weight-for-distance, and with no big improvements by any of the athletes, Bailey—one of the world's top-ranked weight throwers—once again executed great timing and speed as he let the weight fly from his grasp. His throw was poetry in motion as it sailed far and beyond the marks of his rivals, stamping his final seal of dominance with a distance of 45' 5-1/2" for the well-deserved victory.

56-lb. weight-over-the-bar

After three events the athletes retired for a much-needed lunch break, and then resumed competition in the main grandstand area in front of a packed crowd of more than twenty-five thousand cheering fans. The championships resumed with the 56-lb. weight-over-the-bar. The opening height was 14', which all cleared easily, and was then moved up to 15', where we saw MacKay and Price as the first to fall by the wayside.

Harrison Bailey III clobbered the field in the 56-lb. weight-for-distance, upping his distance on each of his three throws, ending with a winning margin of roughly 1-1/2 ft.

With the bar now at 16', only Betz and McKim cleared on their first attempts, but they were joined soon after by Frasure and Bailey. Unfortunately for Vierra, Rider, and Sorin, they exited the competition early to join Price and MacKay. With the bar raised to the height of 17', Bailey and Frasure were first to clear, with Betz also advancing with them on his second attempt. Regrettably, McKim exited the competition to join the others on the sidelines. A special note must be made that McKim kept with the traditional style of the standing throw throughout the competition, as opposed to the spinning method which gives an advantage of 3' to 4'.

With the bar now at the height of 18', Frasure and Bailey cleared on their first attempts, with Betz using all three of his attempts to stay in the competition. Unfortunately he, too, struck out, along with Pockoski—leaving Bailey and Frasure to battle it out.

The bar was set at the new height of 18' 6" which, if cleared by either Bailey or Frasure, would establish a new ground record. After a hard day's throwing, though, this proved too much for the tartan warriors, although they came very close to clearing the height.

After their three attempts were used, it was later declared a draw between the two.

Caber toss

The final event of the first day's competition was the 19' 2" and 119' aggregate caber. This proved a real challenge, with only four athletes able to successfully toss this tyrant of a caber. In the first round, the big Englishman Scott Rider was the first with a turn of 11:00 for the early lead. This lead was short-lived, however, as Dan McKim then turned an 11:30 to go ahead of the Englishman.

In the second round, the challenge heated up with Bailey now masterfully conjuring up a 12:00 toss which put him firmly in the driver's seat. Rider produced a great attempt with 85 degrees; and then Vierra came to life and joined the elite few to toss this robust caber with a 2:15.

In the final round, once more Rider thrilled the multitudes with an 11:45 toss, which moved him into second position, the only man so far to have two successful attempts with this caber. With one last attempt for McKim, all eyes were focused on him. This is a man who is known as one of the strongest with a caber when he is on his form, and he is more than capable of pulling out a 12:00 toss when needed.

As McKim walked to the caber, he looked very composed. He picked up the caber in one clean swoop and set out on his run. As he stopped fast, he seemed to let the caber come off the shoulder a split-second before pulling, lining up the caber for that perfect 12 o'clock. It looked to be on course from his positioning, but just failed in its going over—so close with an 89-degree attempt.

> IT LOOKED TO BE ON COURSE FROM HIS POSITIONING, BUT JUST FAILED IN ITS GOING OVER—SO CLOSE WITH AN 89-DEGREE ATTEMPT.

Overall, Bailey landed in first place with his perfect single toss at 12:00. In second place was Rider with 11:45, and in third McKim with 11:30.

After day one the points looked very interesting with Bailey in the lead overall:

1. Harrison Bailey III   14.5
2. Sean Betz   17
3. Daniel McKim   22
4. Mike Pockoski   25
5. Scott Rider   25.5
6. Eric Frasure   27.5
7. Bert Sorin   31
8. Ryan Vierra   33
9. Rusty Price   39
10. Lucais MacKay   42

17-lb. open stone
Sunday morning's second and final day of competition brought with it an enthusiastic group of athletes looking to get back into the action and pull in the points. In the opening event—the 17-lb. open stone— my focus was directed toward Scott Rider, one of the world's best stone-putters on the international circuit. Looking at him during warm-ups, he appeared to be more comfortable than he did with the 28-lb. Braemar stone on the first day of competition.

Daniel McKim put his head down, ran, stopped, and launched the caber— and the result was a good reason to celebrate.

In the first round Frasure looked a bit nervous at the trig and fouled out on his opening attempt. Price, a winner of the World Stone Putting Championships, was up next and looked totally in the zone—he could possibly give Rider a run for his money in his favorite event—and opened up with a putt of 49' 11".

Next up was Rider who, looking ready to blast this stone into orbit, ripped an awesome throw of 54' 11-1/2" to take the lead.

> NEXT UP WAS RIDER WHO, LOOKING READY TO BLAST THIS STONE INTO ORBIT, RIPPED AN AWESOME THROW OF 54' 11-1/2" TO TAKE THE LEAD.

He's the Englishman who won at Braemar and who has been on an Olympic team in the bobsleigh and at the Commonwealth Games as a shot putter, so winning the open stone was just another day on the job for Scott Rider.

In the second round Betz pulled well up with a putt of 49' 4". Price had a putt of 50' 3". With no real pressure on Rider, he once again demonstrated why he is the world's number one ranked stone putter, unleashing a throw of 55' 10" that gained cheers and applause from the spectators and also his comrades.

In the third round we did see a few improvements with MacKay wrenching out a 48' 1/4" throw and McKim upping his mark with a putt of 51' 2-1/2". Unfortunately for Rider, he fouled out on his last attempt with a massive putt. He was more than happy with his first win of the championships with an unparalleled putt of 55' 10". In second place was McKim with 51' 2-1/2", and Price finished third with 50' 3".

22-lb. (heavy) hammer
Going into the final leg of the IHGF World Hammer Championships, it was tough to pick a winner as points were tight and some pressure was beginning to show during the warm-ups. In the first day's competition with the 16-lb. hammer, Bert Sorin was looking hungry and very eager to win this title, so I tipped him despite what appeared to be a nagging leg injury.

In the first round with the 22-lb. hammer, Price was first up, but he did not make any real impact with his opening throw of only 89'. Rider could only manage a throw of 89' 3". Sorin went next and was the first over the 100' mark with 102' 6". He was followed by Bailey with 104' 9-1/2", McKim with 102' 3", Pockoski with 107' 1/2", and Frasure with 105' 7-1/2". Now things were heating up, but I would have expected a lot more athletes over the 100' mark in the first round.

> RAPIDLY MAKING UP SOME LOST GROUND WAS POCKOSKI WITH A VERY DYNAMIC THROW OF 113' 8".

The second round saw Rider improving with 102' 6", Vierra with 100' 8", Bailey with 107' 3", and Betz with 109' 5". Rapidly making up some lost ground was Pockoski with a very dynamic throw of 113' 8".

Now we had the makings of a riveting competition that would come down to the last round for the IHGF World Hammer Throwing Championships title.

All eyes were now on Sorin, who at this point needed to stay within one foot of Pockoski if he were to stand any chance of claiming the world title. As Sorin began his wind up, he let rip with a loud cry and a look that willed the hammer on before it plummeted to the ground. By the angle it looked to be close to Pockoski's distance, but upon measurement it was not. Although he had improved to a distance of 108' 2", he now knew he had lost his chance for the title—he was looking to hold on to second position overall.

Eric Frasure in his final attempt moved up to third place with 111' 5". Betz also improved on his final attempt, which pulled him up into second position with 112' 1". The highlight was Pockoski once again producing the goods when it mattered most, with an enthralling throw of 115' 5" to claim the title of 2009 IHGF World Hammer Throwing champion.

28-lb. (light) weight-for-distance
With one last event in the U.S. Invitational Championships, the points could not have been closer between Betz and Bailey. The 28-lb. weight-for-distance would be the decider, and the many fans who sat in the bleachers were watching and cheering on their favorite athletes during their warm-ups.

In the first round, Bailey set the mark for Sean to beat with 80' 8". Betz surpassed that with 81' 1/2" and Rider closed in the rear with 79' 2-1/2".

In the second round, however, the tables turned, with Bailey now in the driver's seat with 82' 3-1/2", Betz slightly improving with 81' 5-1/2", and McKim moving into third place with a distance of 79' 9".

In the final round we did see some dramatic improvements from all, but it was still Bailey who was the king of the swingers with a throw of 83' for the win in this event. Betz held on to second place with 81' 5-1/2", and Vierra came up from behind into third with 81' 1-1/2".

It had been a very close competition between both Betz and Bailey and it came down to the final event. Bailey needed to win, which he did, but Betz placed well—and high enough—to secure his win of the overall U.S. Championships.

Asking Betz how he felt as everything came down to the last event, he said, "I knew I had to win, or at least stay close to Harrison, in order to have a chance of claiming this title. This has been a very hard competition and a hard year for most of the athletes, having to peak for the IHGF World Team Championships in Canada and then the week after for the World Championships in Scotland during the central point of the Games season. On top of that, you are trying to sustain that high standard throughout the remainder of the season. I am very happy with the win, and I take my hat off to all my compatriots and especially to Harrison Bailey, who put up an excellent performance throughout the whole Championships."

Asking Bailey if he was happy with the way everything went, he said, "I am very happy with my overall performances, yes—this is the highest I have ever placed at these Championships. Now I am looking forward to training

Where's Waldo? If he's on board this light hammer Mike Pockoski sent flying, look up.

2008 Highland Games world champion Sean Betz is always in the hunt for top honors, and when he won the Braemar stone, the saying An inch is as good as a mile told the story.

this winter and I plan on improving my throwing for next year's season of Games— hopefully it will be my turn to take this title home."

2009 Pleasanton Highland Games Final Results	
1. Sean Betz	25 points
2. Harrison Bailey III	27.5
3. Daniel McKim	33
4. Eric Frasure	38.5
5. Mike Pockoski	41
6. Scott Rider	41
7. Ryan Vierra	50.5
8. Bert Sorin	55.5
9. Rusty Price	61
10. Lucais MacKay	67

The Championships were indeed a battle of nerves and fatigue for Bert Sorin with his badly swollen calf and knee; despite this, he battled on through the whole competition. He was later seen by one of the A-group athletes, Dr. Ed Green, who thought that based on his symptoms Bert could actually be suffering from a blood clot. This was later verified to be the case by Sorin's own doctor. Sorin indicated that he will be on medication for a while, but will make a full recovery and can't wait to resume training for next year's season. We will just have to wait and see what a revitalized Sorin can bring forth to the competition arena next year. M

Fringe

Steven Helmicki

Why the fringes are
Powerlifters considered
The odd
The assisted
The juiced
No credibility
For anything goes
Say what to you
Seven-hundred pound benches
Not on television
Or canvas
But in canvass
And a seamstresses touch
Let the times take
Over with the knowledge
That the great equipment-less
Ancestors of the marathon
Not twenty-six miles
But nine lifts
In the bare flesh
Were a different machine
Like the greatest generation
Look through the glass
Of a simpler time
There really is no fair way
To compare the past
Or the future
With the present technology
Of extra-wide stances
Stomach presses
Three-plied
Protection for such
An awkward groove
But I watched it with my own eyes
And sacrificed my body for its lust
Full heaviness
Believe me we feel
That you can only be
Compared against
Your time.
And the knowledge it felt
Heavy to all of us.

M

Harnessing the
The Power of Placebo

Brian Jones, Ph.D.

Author of *The Complete Sandbag Training Course, The Conditioning Handbook: Getting In Top Shape,* and *Grappling Basics: A New Twist on Conditioning*

Few activities highlight the mind–body connection like heavy lifting. All serious lifters recognize the importance mindset, mood, motivation, and belief when it comes to breaking PRs and pushing through tough workouts. Without the belief that you can move the bar, the courage to try, and the steadfastness to fight through the tough reps, you won't get very far with your training. It seems that in the past few years, science has been confirming experimentally what athletes have known all along.

The placebo effect is a well-known phenomenon in scientific research. It refers to physiological changes caused by inert substances or treatments. For instance, if a company were testing a new anti-inflammatory pill, there would be three different groups—a control group, a drug group, and a placebo group. The control group would receive no treatment of any sort. The drug and placebo groups would both get identical-looking pills, but the drug group's pills would contain the medicine while the placebo group's pill would not. The reason for this design is that some percentage of the placebo group will show improvement from the inert substance. This is known as the placebo effect. The exact causes of the placebo effect are unknown. The effect occurs in nearly all pharmaceutical research and in many cases is nearly as strong as the drug itself.

In 2007 Harvard psychologists Alia Crum and Ellen Langer decided to look at the placebo effect as it applied to exercise. (1) They recruited 84 hotel room attendants and measured a series of health-related variables—bodyweight, blood pressure, body fat, waist-to-hip ratio, and body mass index. The subjects were divided into two groups. Each group had the same level of physical activity. One group was told that their jobs provided the amount of physical activity recommended by the Surgeon General for an active lifestyle; the other was told nothing. After 4 weeks the two groups were retested. Those subjects who thought they were getting enough exercise showed significant improvements in all the health-related variables. This was true even though they had not changed their activity levels. It seems that the perception of their on-the-job efforts as exercise helped them accrue health benefits.

No one is claiming that you can simply think yourself fit, but your mindset about training may help you maximize the benefits. In a more recent research study, Christopher Beedie (2009) found that athletes are aware of the power of belief on their performances. (2) He found that 97% of those surveyed believed that the placebo effect mattered in competitive sports, and 73% of them could relate personal experiences with it. These findings, he claims, point to the need for further research into the placebo effect and sports performance.

A third study by Duncan et al., which demonstrates how the mind can exert powerful influences on performance, was published in the *International Journal of Sports Physiology and Performance* in 2009. (3) Subjects were told they would be given either a drink containing caffeine or a placebo drink prior to exercise. In reality, neither drink had caffeine. But those who thought they had received caffeine were able to perform a significantly higher number of leg extension repetitions. Consider the effects a few more reps per set might have over six months or a year of training.

> NO ONE IS CLAIMING THAT YOU CAN SIMPLY THINK YOURSELF FIT, BUT YOUR MINDSET ABOUT TRAINING MAY HELP YOU MAXIMIZE THE BENEFITS.

How can we harness this phenomenon to boost our performances? The first application has to do with the power of belief in the effectiveness of the training. The trainee has to truly believe that his training methods are effective. He has to convince himself that each workout session is vital, each recovery period is essential, and all the exercises are purposeful. In a properly designed training schedule this will be true anyway. Eliminate extraneous movements and make sure that each piece of the program is a proven method of achieving your goal. It is okay to experiment with new methods, but avoid jumping on the bandwagon of every passing fad. Go basic and go hard.

If you are a coach, you need to stress to your athletes the importance of each training exercise. Tell them precisely why they are doing it and how it will help their performance. Good coaches should be skeptical. Although they may have some reservations about methods they are implementing for the first time, these concerns should never be expressed in front of the athletes. As a coach your job is to teach and motivate. State in no uncertain terms that if your athletes follow your program, they will get stronger and fitter.

As the study by Beedie demonstrated, most athletes have already experienced the placebo effect during competition or practice; thus, there exists a real potential to exploit it. One of the most common methods is the use of pre-performance rituals. Take time to develop your own rituals to help you get into your state of optimal arousal. Most lifters have a specific routine for approaching and setting up before heavy attempts. Others may have a word or phrase that they focus on internally or even yell aloud. Finally, many use such substances as ammonia capsules or have a training partner smack them in order to elicit an adrenaline surge. As silly as they may seem to spectators who are not athletes, these rituals may mean the difference between success and failure on the platform. Each ritual will be and should be individual. Develop rituals for yourself and encourage the athletes you train to do the same. For obvious reasons these rituals should always be kept within the bounds of safety.

Experienced strength coaches often have their own techniques for breaking through mental barriers. Intentionally overloading the bar is one such example. Many times progress plateaus are, in whole or in part, mental blocks. An athlete may get stuck at a certain weight and be unable to move beyond it. Coaches have been known to place slightly more weight on the bar than the athlete thinks is there. The athlete is deceived into believing he is lifting a weight that is within his capacity. This confidence allows him to lift a weight he might otherwise have missed. Of course, it is important to only add a little more weight. A lifter with a max squat of 500 lb. might move an extra 5 or 10 lb., but 550 lb. would still crush him.

> THE POINT IS THAT YOUR BELIEFS ABOUT YOUR TRAINING MATTER, AND THEY MATTER IN TANGIBLE WAYS.

The point is that your beliefs about your training matter, and they matter in tangible ways. The placebo effect can just as easily have negative consequences. Consider an athlete with a defeatist attitude or low self-esteem. This lack of confidence will result in a self-fulfilling prophecy. These psycho–physical interactions are happening all the time, and it is the wise coach or athlete who will recognize and direct them rather than being at their mercy. **M**

References
1. A. J. Crum and E. J. Langer, "Mind-set matters: exercise and the placebo effect," *Psychol Sci.* 18 (2): 165–171 (2009).
2. C. J. Beedie, "Placebo effects in competitive sport: qualitative data," *J Sport Sci Med.* 6 (2007): 21–28.
3. M. J. Duncan, M. Lyons, and J. Hankey, "Placebo effects of caffeine on short-term resistance exercise to failure," *Int J Sports Physiol Perform.* 4 (2): 244–253 (2009).

The Iron Mine

Equipment

Adjustable Grippers
and strength training equipment. Chest crusher, front squat harness, and more. www.gripempire.com.

Strength Equipment
from the FIRST to close the No. 3 Captains of Crush Gripper. Custom super-duty racks, benches and selectorized machines by Sorinex. Owned, designed and tested to be virtually bombproof by Richard Sorin. 16 years of experience supplying universities, gyms and serious lifters nationwide. Call and talk with The Grip Man at 877-767-4639, P.O. Box 121, Irmo, SC 29063; visit our website at www.sorinex.com and see our training tips section!

Atlas Stone Molds from Slater's!
Easy to make, hard to break, heavy-duty poly-Lexan, for time-after-time uses in 8, 10, 12, 14, 16, 18, 20, & 24-inch dia. Low int'l & dom. S&H. 740-654-2204. E-mail steve@slatershardware.com; dealers: www.slatershardware.com, www.totalperformancesports.com, www.marunde-muscle.com, www.prowriststraps.com.

Free Catalog: IronMind Enterprises Tools of the Trade for Serious Strength Athletes
IronMind is the home of Captains of Crush® Grippers, *SUPER SQUATS*, Just Protein®, *MILO®*, the Vulcan Racks II+ System Squat Racks, Strong-Enough Lifting Straps™, and the Draft Horse Pulling Harness™, not to mention the world's leading line of grip tools, a top-quality line of gym equipment, strongman training equipment for the world's strongest men, and books, posters, and DVDs to inform and inspire you to greater success. While we sell plenty of equipment to champion strength athletes around the world, our specialty is the dedicated home trainer—strong guys who train in their garages, basements and backyards. Come take a look at what we have to offer. P.O. Box 1228, Nevada City, CA 95959 USA; t - 530-272-3579; f – 530-272-3095; website and on-line store: www.ironmind.com; e-mail: sales@iron-mind.com.

Equipment

World-class VULKAN Supports
Heavy-duty, high-quality: knee, arm, back, & pants for strongman, powerlifters, heavy events, bodybuilders. Retail & wholesale. www.theweakgeteaten.com.

Real Wood Strongman Logs
Slater's True Logs are built to last, used in top pro strongman contests. E-mail steve@slatershardware.com, 740-654-2204; www.slatershardware.com.

Strength Equipment/Stone Molds
Nothing but the best strength training/ strongman equipment: harnesses, stone molds, kettlebells, books, DVDs and more. www.totalperformancesports.com. 617-387-5998.

Strong, Pain-Free Hands
In one convenient package: **three** vital training tools and guide for preventing, reducing, or eliminating hand pain. Kit includes IronMind EGG, Expand-Your-Hand Bands, Easy Wrist-Relief Soft Weight, and booklet "How to Develop Strong, Pain-Free Hands." $51.85 + S&H: $13 USA, US$19 Canada, US$40 all others. Available in our on-line store at www.ironmind.com, or send payment to IronMind Enterprises, Inc., P.O. Box 1228, Nevada City, CA 95959 USA.

CoC Key: From Miles to Mils
Trim that gap (between the handles of your Captains of Crush Grippers) and then make it disappear! The CoC Key will help you unlock your next rounds of PRs, giving you a precise way to gauge your progress. How big was that gap, really? With steps of 2, 4, 6, 8, 10, 12, 14 and 16 mm, the CoC Key will tell you exactly where you are . . . which is the first step to getting where you'd rather be. $9.95 + S&H: $4 USA, US$7 Canada, US$13 all others. www.ironmind.com.

IronMind Goods in Germany!
Books, gear, equipment and MORE! www.c-of-c.de, Choice of Champions, Dr. Hermann Korte, Recklinghaeuser Str. 119, 45721 Haltern am See, Germany; e-mail info@k3k.de.

Training: Magazines, Books, DVDs

"The Steel Tip Newsletter"
by Dr. Ken is once again available. www.oldtimestrongman.com. 1-800-978-0206.

NEW! Battling Ropes DVD
Featuring Ingrid Marcum, champion weightlifter and Olympic bobsled team hopeful, this DVD shows you how to build strength and stamina using the unique Battling Ropes system developed by John Brookfield. Aimed at both individuals and teams, the system uses a long, heavy rope to train at high levels of intensity for longer durations, increasing your ability to generate and sustain power. Strongmen, football players, Special Forces types especially, you'll want this. 48 min., NTSC. $39.95 plus S&H: $5/US; $7/Can; $13/all others; www.ironmind.com.

Weightlifting Videos
20 high-quality DVDs from every weight class of the 2006 USA W/L Nat. Jr. Champs & Pan-Am Qualifier, $30/session; e-mail: WeightliftingVideoDirect@gmail.com for compressed samples or to order.

Real Strength Real Muscle
This article anthology by the late Coach John Christy is for Real People with Real Lives: those who want to get bigger, stronger, and better conditioned without sacrificing family, school, or work. Real routines, real trainees, real answers, real nutritional guidance. 408 pp. $46.50 ppd. USA / US$71.50 ppd. others. DVDs also available. Order from www.realstrength-realmuscle.com/book.htm.

Updated! *Captains of Crush Grippers* **book**
Whether you want to get an A+ on your next gripper exam or only care about building a stronger grip, you'll want to get this book—now updated and expanded to include over 45% new material, and most of it on training. Dedicated to all who know "it's not a crush . . . it's an obsession!" 192 pp. $19.95 + S&H: $5.00 USA, US$7.00 Can., US$13.00 all others. IronMind Enterprises, www.ironmind.com.

The Iron Mine

Training: Magazines, Books, DVDs

Paul Anderson's Books and Tapes
The Paul Anderson Youth Home offers a free catalog of Paul's books and tapes, as well as the Coleman video on Paul's life. This gives you a unique opportunity to learn from the world's strongest man while helping to support the youth home which Paul Anderson was dedicated to building. For a copy of this catalog, contact: Paul Anderson Youth Home, P. O. Box 525, Vidalia, GA 30345, e-mail: info@payh.org.

Powerlifting USA
Contest results, schedules, training. 12 iss/year; $36.95 US; $96.00 elsewhere. PLUSA, P. O. Box 467, Camarillo, CA 93011.

The Get-Big-and-Strong Program
SUPER SQUATS: *How to Gain 30 Pounds of Muscle in 6 Weeks:* This is the program that has turned human toothpicks into stalwarts and stalwarts into legends. After a few minutes under a squat bar, you will find out what you're made of: and if you want to get bigger and stronger and have no use for drugs, fancy equipment, or the latest food supplement fad, this is your book. 112 pp. $16.95 plus S&H: $5/US; $7/Can; $13/all others; www.ironmind.com.

Steve Justa's "High Plains Heavy Metal IronMaster's Bible"
No bull, strength-building tips. 20 big pages, big lifts, big poses, over 40 photos. Send $20.00 to Steve Justa, Box 97, Harvard, NE 68944.

Be Your Best by David Morgan
Crosstraining for CrossFit's King Kong? Author and Olympian weightlifter Morgan smashed the CrossFit King Kong record in his first attempt—and with 275/500 instead of 250/455 in the clean and DL. Want to be strong and fit? You'll want his book on training to be your best. 128 pp. $19.95 + S&H: $7.00 USA/US$10.00 Can/US$16.00 others. www.ironmind.com.

Starr Novel
The Susquehanna River Hills Chronicles, a novel by Bill Starr. $20 + $6 S&H USA; 1011 Warwick Drive, #3-C, Aberdeen, MD 21001.

Training: Magazines, Books, DVDs

Free Illustrated Catalog!
Books, courses, back-date magazines, out-of-prints, new, etc. Classic how-to training methods and biographies by all the old masters. Buy, sell, trade, collecting over 25 years. Bill Hinbern, 32430-E Cloverdale, Farmington, MI 48336; www.superstrengthbooks.com.

Denis Reno's Newsletter
The quickest and best way to get Olympic weightlifting results, from local contests to World Championships. $26/year US, $30 Can., $45–$50 others. Denis Reno, 30 Cambria Road, Newton, MA 02165; e-mail: renoswlnl@verizon.net.

Defying Gravity
by Bill Starr. Signed. Hard cover $20, soft cover $15 + $4.00 S&H. Bill Starr, 1011 Warwick Drive, #3-C, Aberdeen, MD 21001.

World Weightlifting
The official magazine of the International Weightlifting Federation; its four issues a year cover contests worldwide. $40/year Europe, $50 elsewhere. World Weightlifting, IWF Secretariat, 1146 Budapest, Istvanmezei ut 1-3, Hungary.

Websites, Training Forums

The IronMind News
The Strength World's News Source. Fast. Accurate. Objective. www.ironmind.com.

Captains of Crush Grippers Fans
The facts, fiction, myths about Captains of Crush Grippers, and more: training programs, history highlights, gripper glossary, how-tos & FAQs—it's all here. www.captainsofcrushgrippers.com.

Sustain Strength & Speed
Battling Ropes: you read about them in *MILO.* Learn more about John Brookfield's strength and conditioning system at www.battlingropes.com.

PrimordialStrengthSystems.com
Creating the most explosive athletes through the science of persistence.

Websites, Training Forums

Strong and Healthy Hands for Everyone
www.strongandhealthyhands.com.

Strengthcoach.tv
For trainees and coaches—advancing the fundamental, creative, and limitless potential of strength development methodology.

Associations

Join USA Weightlifting!
The National Governing Body for the Olympic sport. Go to www.usaweightlifting.org or call 719-866-4508, for news about recent competitions and courses, membership information, local and national events, coaching education, and the newest items available on-line. Membership benefits include participant accident insurance, a subscription to *Weightlifting, USA,* and **super discounts** on airline tickets, hotels, car rentals, and other products and services through our Olympic partnership!

The Association of Oldetime Barbell & Strongmen
A not-to-be-missed annual reunion and dinner—this year, it's on October 23, 2010—for some of the biggest names in the Iron Game. Members receive a very interesting newsletter. Annual donation is $25, payable to AOBS, c/o Artie Drechsler, President, 33-30 – 150th Street, Flushing, NY 11354; email: lifttech@earthlink.net; www.wlinfo.com.

The Iron Mine

Looking to buy or sell? Want to give your upcoming contest an extra boost? Advertise in the Iron Mine. $10 per line per insertion, no minimum number of lines. No display ads, please. All material subject to approval. Send advertising copy or direct questions to: *MILO,* P.O. Box 1228, Nevada City, CA 95959, tel: 530-272-3579, fax: 530-272-3095, sales@ironmind.com. *We try to screen the advertising, but let the buyer beware.*

128 MILO | Mar. 2010, Vol. 17, No. 4